Finding Work as a Close Protection Specialist (Bodyguard)

2015 - 2016 Updated Edition

Published by Robin Barratt
© Robin Barratt 2015, and all the authors herein
ISBN: 978-1515398325

All rights reserved. No part of this publication may be reproduced,
distributed, or transmitted in any form or by any means,
including photocopying, recording, or other electronic or mechanical methods,
without the prior written permission of the publisher,
except in the case of brief quotations embodied in critical reviews and
certain other non-commercial uses permitted by copyright law.
For permission requests, email the publisher at the address below.

W: www.RobinBarrattPublishing.com
E: Robin@RobinBarrattPublishing.com
E: RobinBarratt@yahoo.com

Camberford
LAW PLC

INNOVATIVE INSURANCE

INNOVATIVE INSURANCE for the
CLOSE PROTECTION INDUSTRY

Camberford Law have been established since 1958 and over the years we have developed a thorough and specialised knowledge of insurances relating to all types of organisations in the Security Industry.

For many years we have provided a specialist scheme for the Close Protection industry.

COVER CAN INCLUDE

- Employers' Liability
- Public Liability including Efficacy
- Life Assurance
- Legal Expenses
- Personal Accident Cover including Medical and Repatriation Expenses
- Kidnap and Ransom

BENEFITS

- Fast turnaround on Quotations
- Proposal Forms available online
- Documentation issued in-house
- Competitive Prices
- Instalment Plan available

FREDA WEST or AMY WILLS

follow us @camberfordlaw

T 020 8315 5000
E closeprotection@camberfordlaw.com
www.camberfordlaw.com/closeprotection

Insurance Brokers . Underwriting Agents . Lloyd's Brokers

Authorised and Regulated by the Financial Conduct Authority

PRINCIPLE SPONSOR

CAMBERFORD LAW

A leading insurance broker specialising in insurance for the security and protection industries. Camberford Law PLC have been in Insurance since 1958 and over the years we have developed a thorough and specialised knowledge of Insurances relating to all types of organizations in the Security Industry. We are perhaps the leading Insurance Brokers to the Security Industry and our arrangements are utilised by numerous companies and individuals in every part of the Country. As an extension of our main scheme for the Security Industry, we have developed exclusive and specialized arrangements providing comprehensive and unique world wide cover for close and personal protection companies and individuals. We can provide specialised cover at competitive terms for the following Insurances:

- Employers' Liability
- Public Liability
- Personal Accident

W: **www.camberfordlaw.com**

CONTRIBUTORS

Robin Barratt
Robin has small publishing company and has been writing and publishing since the year 2000, after stepping away from security operations and training; an industry he was in for almost twenty years previously. He is a genre best-selling author of six non-fiction true crime books (*Doing the Doors, Confessions of a Doorman, Bouncers and Bodyguards, Respect and Reputation, Mammoth Book of Hard Bastards* and *Britain's Toughest Women*) as well as a large number of Kindle books on a range of topics and subjects. He founded and published *Tough Talk*, an acclaimed online magazine interviewing martial artists, boxers, combat specialists etc., and also founded *The Circuit* magazine for the British Bodyguard Association, and published the *International Directory of Security & Close Protection* for Varsity Publications. He has written hundreds of articles for magazines and newspapers worldwide, the author of one biography, three self-help guides and two travel anthologies about Bahrain where he lived for four years, and where he was also commissioned to produce and publish a quality book for one of the biggest Arab merchant families in the Gulf region.
E: RobinBarratt@yahoo.com
W: www.RobinBarrattPublishing.com

Tony Scotti
For forty years Tony Scotti has catered to the training needs of industry and public service agencies. He has trained governments, corporations, law enforcement agencies and military organizations to avoid vehicle violence. Going on his 5th decade his training programs have been conducted in over thirty-eight countries, and he has trained students from sixty-four countries and conducted training programs on five continents. He has combined his experience working in High Risk Areas and his engineering skills, (He holds a B.S. in Engineering from Northeastern University, USA) to pioneer most of the concepts

used in Security Driver Training. His programs blend the science of vehicle dynamics with first-hand experience gained while conducting real world security operations in moderate and high risk locales around the globe. The end result has been teaching students the critical skills needed to survive a life threatening situation while behind the wheel.
E: TonyScotti@msn.com
W: www.VehicleDynamics.com
F: www.facebook.com/tony.scotti.7

Tyrrel Francis
Tyrrel Francis started judo and karate at the age of thirteen. In 1991 he joined the Royal Navy and served with Commando Helicopter Force, operating in the Former Yugoslavia in the mid-'90s, and in the Gulf in the early 2000s, as well as supporting the Royal Marines on various training detachments in places such as Norway, Holland and the United States. Still practising martial arts today, Tyrrel holds a 2nd Dan in Shotokan karate, and a 3rd Degree in freestyle kickboxing, but has now progressed to Muay Thai, and competes on the K1 circuit (*K1 is a kickboxing platform and martial arts brand, well-known worldwide mainly for its heavyweight division fights*). Passionate about writing, as well as martial arts, Tyrrel has trained with high-ranking and top-rated martial arts instructors in arts such as Ju-jitsu, American Kempo, Aikido, Jeet Kung Do, and of course, Muay Thai and karate. Being a martial artist, self-defence has always been a topic of interest for Tyrrel fuelled, at times, by witnessing, or hearing about first-hand, the situations that friends over the years have either caused, contributed to, or fallen foul of. His first book *Personal Safety & Self Defence - A practical guide to avoiding and dealing with conflict* (ISBN: 978-1514889855) is out now in paperback and Kindle.
F: www.Facebook.com/tyrrelfrancis

Lawrence Snow
Lawrence Snow has spent over twenty years in the security business and is a leader in providing online marketing solutions

for small to mid-sized security and executive protection businesses.
W: www.LarrySnow.me

Freda West
Freda West, Senior Account Executive with Camberford Law, a leading insurance broker specialising in insurance for the security and protection industries. Camberford Law are members of the British Security Industry Association Ltd (BSIA) and International Professional Security Association.
T: 44 (0) 20 8315 5022
E: FredaW@CamberfordLaw.com
W: www.CamberfordLaw.com

Mo Teague
Mo is the Founder of Hard Target Combat System, a Close Quarter Combat system which Mo has taught to Military, Law Enforcement, Close Protection and Security Officers worldwide including the Middle East. Mo is also a Jeet Kune Do instructor under Grand Master Richard Bustillo, and was in 2012 was honoured in the Martial Arts Hall of Fame.
E: MoTeague@hotmail.co.uk

Richard Pendry
Richard spent his formative years in the Parachute Regiment where he learned the art of soldiering in one of the world's most elite units. Using his military skills he entered into the elusive world of Private Security, working in Iraq, Africa, Syria and Afghanistan. Over the last decade he has been at the tip of the spear, experiencing at first hand the effects of the might of the Western military machine and its attempt to win the War on Terror. Richard has studied Security & Risk Management at the world renown Scarmen Centre of Criminology, Leicester University, and is currently reading a masters degree in Terrorism, at St Andrew's University Centre for the Study Political Violence & Terrorism. As a freelance consultant he worked for many organisations and is always looking for the next

challenging assignment. His new book *Damascus Road* is out shortly.
E: Richard@RichardCPendry.com
W: www.www.RichardCPendry.com

Timm Smith
Advocate Timm Smith, CEO of Ronin SA holds degrees in Law and Philosophy as well as qualifications as a Paramedic in both the UK and South Africa. Despite being admitted as one of South Africa's youngest barristers he felt that his calling was the provision of quality close protection - given a misspent youth, as he calls it - working his way through university as a doorman. He credits his successes within the CP industry, over the last twenty years, to the grounding he received from the likes of Dennis Martin and Lofty Wiseman of CQB Services, Bob Duggan of ESI, and his Commanding Officers within the Specialized Policing Units he has served within in South Africa, both as a bodyguard and tactical medic. In 2005 he was called on to Chair the National Standards Generating Committee which wrote the national standards in close protection for Police, Intelligence , Military and civilian sectors. These standards are still used today. Driven by the principle of delivering excellence by choice, Ronin SA committed itself to training quality Close Protection Operators and Remote Medics from its inception in 1995. By way of distinction from the rest of the industry, Ronin SA has always held the view that a complete Close Protection Operator should have both tactical and medical competencies to honestly fulfil their client's expectations. This is based on the simple observation that a client legitimately expects to stay alive in your presence, being protected from any threat, be it an attack, accident or personal medical emergency. If you want to do something different and become something more that does not involve a tick-in-a-box, we would like to meet you.
E: ContactUs@Ronin.co.za
W: www.Ronin.co.za

Shaun West

Shaun is a highly experienced Close Protection Operative and Security Consultant. Shaun's current roles include being CEO of Shaun West Associates and a director within the British Bodyguard Association. Shaun has extensive security experience gained through working on a global platform, within both cityscape corporate environments and remote hostile settings. Before joining the security industry, Shaun served with the Elite Parachute Regiment and its specialist components carrying out numerous operational tours, before going onto complete one of the most highly rated bodyguard courses worldwide. Through Shaun West Associates, Shaun's vision of bringing the 'best of the best' under one company banner and delivering exceptional services that transcend the offerings of traditional providers now exists. Shaun is the operational hub of the company and remains at the 'coal face' of its service delivery and selection criteria. Shaun's work with the British Bodyguard Association has helped to grow the organisation, working within a close-knit team to help transform the association and its offerings to enable hundreds of its members to benefit from the services on offer; services which help to greatly increase and develop an individuals professional capacity. Shaun has also written numerous articles for publications worldwide, and is heavily involved with the production of the acclaimed Circuit Magazine and in the creation of an 'industry first' insurance product.
E: Shaun@The-BBA.org.uk
W: www.The-BBA.org.uk
W : www.ShaunWest.co.uk

Tony Fithon

Tony completed over 20 years service in the British Army and in that time he was involved in many military operations throughout the world, gaining a vast amount of security knowledge and expertise, working at all levels in both hostile and non-hostile environments. After leaving the Army Tony, a 3rd Dan Black Belt in Jeet Kune Do (trained under Peter Constantine), started working in the security industry as a bodyguard now re-titled a

Close Protection Operative (CPO), and during that time he built up a large portfolio of clients including TV celebrities and politicians. He has provided security protection for Prime Ministers Margaret Thatcher and Edward Heath, and many MPs including Lord Dennis Healy and Michael Portillo. Whilst providing security for the Prime Minister of Ethiopia and his family, he had the opportunity to speak with all delegates and Ministers that had travelled with him to London, and since then we have been heavily involved with training for many African students. During his career Tony also provided many covert surveillance operations, for barristers, solicitors, private companies and members of the public, and won a prestigious contract to provide surveillance for the Met Police and the Home Office. Within a short period of time, Tony decided to set up his own security company and since the companies formation in 1993, Tony has been responsible for directing many security contracts, which the company continues with to this day. Drawing from his experiences as an instructor (teacher) whilst serving in the Army, Tony decided to add a Training Centre to Impacts expanding business, and eventually purchased a purposed built training centre in Colchester equipped with state of the art facilities, including a fully equipped gymnasium, along with a 185 acre farm complex in Borden Hampshire, for the more specialised training programmes such as Close Protection Teams, Hostile Environmental and Ship Security Training, to incorporate training and development prior to deployment overseas and hostile environments. Tony also has access to over four thousand acres of training land at the old American air base in Woodbridge Suffolk. During the past twenty years Tony has been very successful tendering and gaining contracts for many large corporate and blue chip companies. His Company ISS Ltd have been the main provider of security personal to Network Rail, for the prevention of expensive materials and copper cable theft. From its success in taking over from another security company on the Eurostar Line and stopping the cable theft, Tony also deployed over 150 security personnel per day on projects for network rail, to deter and stop cable being stolen. Due to his

military tactical experience and exceptional manpower; Tony have been able to ensure that all commissioning dates for the restructure of the line have been met. Tony was then awarded an £8 million contract to deploy security personnel to the West Midlands (Birmingham) which was a major triumph over the bigger security companies within the UK, and was responsible for the security for the West Coast main line during a 200 million pound refit of cable. This led to a substantial contract during the Olympic Games for Security to Highfields at the Olympic Village and Tony was responsible for close protection to all celebrities that visited the games and visits to London. Tony and his team specialise in hostile environment and close protection training for personnel requiring appropriate certification and licensing both in the UK and internationally, and at the moment is very busy delivering Physical and Disengagement training to several Children's Secure Units in the North West, and also delivers Challenging Behaviour, Conflict Management and First Aid Training.
T: Tony@Impact-Security.com
W: www.Impact-Security.com

Ronin™ South Africa

Are You As Unique As This Course?

Market Leaders in Progressive Close Protection and Medical Training

Close Protection Course
Includes Hostile Environment Preparation and the *Level 3 Certificate - Working as a CP Operative within the Private Security Industry*

Remote Medical Technician Course
Includes the UK Ambulance Technician Course
BTEC Level 3 Certificate in Ambulance Aid

You can't honestly call yourself a "Body" "Guard" unless you have completed both Courses
(With a Graduate Discount of course)

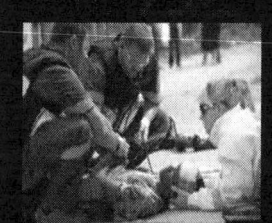

edexcel
advancing learning, changing lives

City & Guilds

www.ronin.co.za

Ronin™ is trademarked within the UK & EU and can only legally be used by Ronin South Africa

CONTENTS

Introduction To The Industry... Page 16
By Robin Barratt
High Risk Close Protection... Page 24
By Richard Pendry
Body + Guard?... Page 31
By Timm Smith
To Join Or Not To Join - The Benefits Of Associations... Page 36
By Shaun West
Deciding On How To Start Your CP Career... Page 40
By Robin Barratt
It's Not Easy Being In Security... Page 44
By Lawrence Snow
Finding The Best CP Training Courses... Page 47
By Robin Barratt
Security Driving And Secure Transportation... Page 54
By Tony Scotti
Finding Work... Page 57
By Robin Barratt
A Female CPOs Journey Into The Industry... Page 65
By El Mitropoulou
International Consultancy... Page 76
By Robin Barratt
Executive Drive Time... Page 81
By Tony Scotti
More On Looking For Work... Page 83
By Robin Barratt
Effective Networking... Page 89
By Robin Barratt
Another Female's Journey Into The Industry... Page 101
By Debbie Mills
Can Door Supervisors Make Good CPOs?... Page 113
By Robin Barratt

How To Write A Good CV... Page 118
By Robin Barratt
How Many CVs Have I Received This Week!... Page 123
By Tony Fithon
Should CPOS Be Trained In CQC?... Page 128
By Robin Barratt
CQC, A Must For The Professional CPO... Page 132
By Tyrell Francis
CQC For Protection Officers... Page 137
By Mo Teague
An Interesting Conversation... Page 141
By Robin Barratt
Certification And Experience... Page 148
By Tony Scotti
Making Sure You Are Insured... Page 150
By Freda West
**Has The Government Failed
The British Close Protection Industry?...** Page 153
By Robin Barratt

ADVERTS

Camberford Law... Page 03
Ronin SA... Page 12
The British Bodyguard Association... Page 15
International Security Driver Association... Page 56

The Dedicated Association For Dedicated Professionals

www.the-bba.org.uk
BRITISH BODYGUARD ASSOCIATION
Call 0191 645 0865 or Email admin@the-bba.org.uk

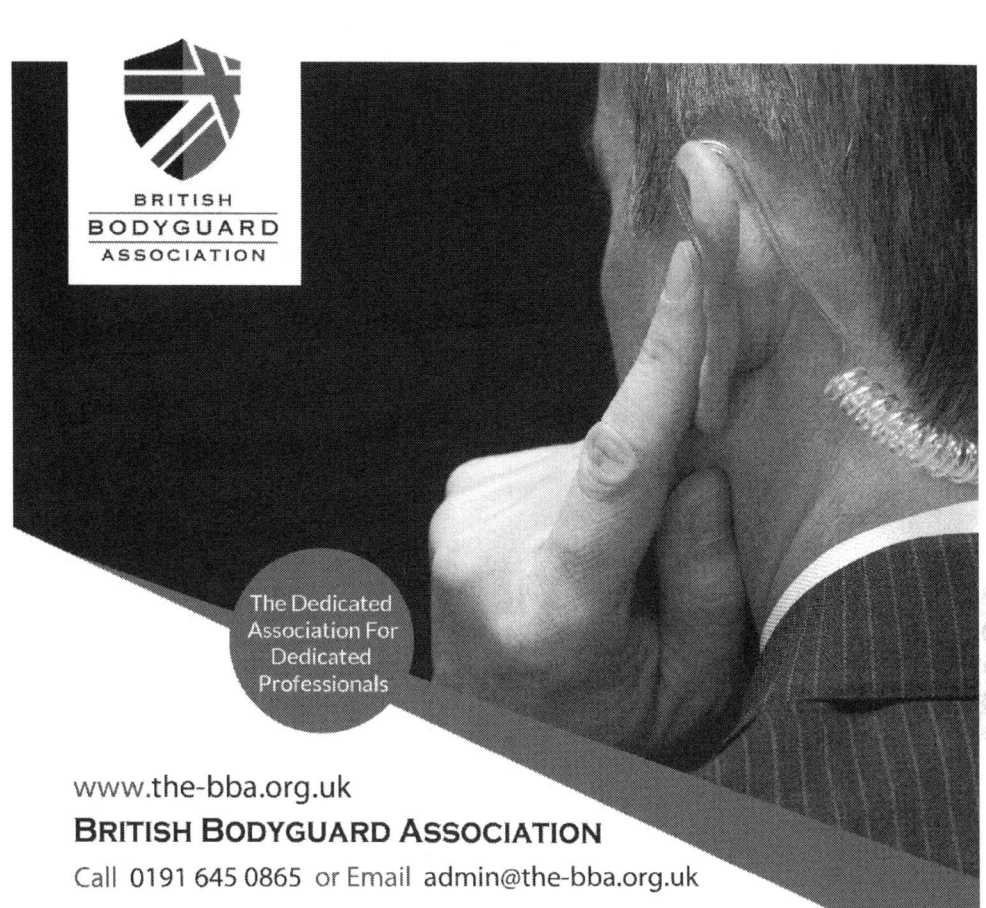

Employment Opportunities
Members get emailed immediately as new positions become available.
The BBA Jobs Board is the largest source of industry jobs relevant to protection specialists.

BBA Networking and Events
Fact: Most security jobs are gained through referral. Extend your professional network by attending association hosted events. Benefit from hearing industry experts and special guests speakers. Network and socialise with peers and industry noteworthy's.

The Circuit Magazine
Stay informed with all the latest news, reviews, advice and opinion. The Circuit is the industries No1 magazine for operators, wrote by operators.

The BBA Brand
Displaying the BBA logo instantly adds credibility through association to one of the idustries most respected organisations. Professionals recognise the BBA brand as a hallmark of quality and excellence.

Specialist Insurance
The BBA and our partners at Lockton have developed an insurance policy which is tailor-made for British bodyguards. This policy is exclusive to the BBA and our Protect members. You cannot get this anywhere else.

CPD Profile
The BBA CPD Profile is the fastest growing career tool for security professionals looking to record their professional development and increase their employability.

INTRODUCTION TO THE INDUSTRY
By Robin Barratt

It is a fact that, for many Close Protection Officers (CPOs), finding work is harder than it has ever been. Not because there is less work out there, in fact the opposite is probably true; with global threat levels at an all-time high, there is more work in the security industry now than there ever has been. But because there are now thousands more so-called 'qualified' CPOs chasing after each and every position. At the time of updating this manual for 2015, in the UK alone there are 15,226 Security Industry Authority (SIA) valid licences. Yes, over fifteen thousand people in the UK have taken and passed a close protection course and have their license to operate! But there are definitely not 15,226 people working in this sector; it is a sad fact that most people with a Security Industry Authority badge have never actually done a days close protection work in their lives!

However, although there are certain facts and feelings that circulate within the protection industry that really must be aired, this is not a personal rant about how the SIA has ruined the close protection industry in the UK; a sentiment shown by almost every veteran CPO, as well as every former military and police protection officer I have met and talked to over the years, including RMP and SF. My ranting about the SIA won't change a thing, but me giving you some tips and hints and suggestions about how to increase your chances of work in this industry, just might.

Before SIA licensing, one protection based position would have probably attracted ten to fifteen high-quality, experienced applicants. Now literally hundreds apply for every single position and if you don't have the right background, the right training or the right experience, your CV is unlikely to even get looked at, let alone get yourself invited for an interview. Sad but true. Before, even if you were not successful, you were still likely to get a polite reply from the employers and agencies, thanking you for your application. Now most employers and agencies don't bother to reply (security employment agencies are definitely the worst for this!).

Before SIA licensing, the close protection industry was selective, discreet and understandably fairly elitist - it had to be, as ultimately the job could involve protecting someone's life. But now virtually anyone can train and get an SIA license to protect; all you need to do now is just to pay your money and turn up for your course! That is just about it! Simple. Back in the '80s and '90s training was tough, demanding and unforgiving, and only the very best of the best would pass and go onto a career in this specialised and demanding sector of security. Now there is rarely a fail and many CP training companies actually have a money back guarantee; they will pass you because they want to market and sell their courses linked to 100% pass rates! Hard to believe but it's absolutely true. Before the SIA, training was extremely practical, with drills practised over and over and over again, until perfect. Now, for many companies, training is mainly classroom based because they want to run the course in as short time as possible, to cut costs and increase profitability. According to the SIA, all CP courses should take a minimum of 138 hours - which in theory means that if you train for 12 hours a day, you can complete your course in just under 11 days straight. How can people learn everything that is needed in close protection in just 11 days? When I trained, it took three to four days just to master embuss and debuss procedures; we practised over and over and over again, for hours upon hours every day. But not now. According to the SIA website, an accredited course should cover; Roles and Responsibilities of the Close Protection Operative, Threat and Risk Assessment, Surveillance Awareness, Operational Planning, Law and Legislation, Interpersonal Skills, Close Protection Teamwork and Briefing, Conduct Reconnaissance, Close Protection Foot Drills, Route Selection, Close Protection Journey Management, Search Procedures, Incident Management and Venue Security. The Conflict Management Module should cover; Avoiding Conflict and Reducing Personal Risk, Defusing Conflict, Resolving and

Learning from Conflict, Application of Communication Skills and Conflict Management for Security Guarding and Close Protection. In 138 hours. I mean... seriously! But because of this, every wannabe - regardless of aptitude and attitude - with a couple of grand and two weeks spare - can get a British Government license to, quite possibly, protect the life of another human being. The Police Service has strict admission criteria, extensive training and a rigorous pass or fail policy. The Fire Brigade and Paramedics are the same; yet the close protection industry in the UK has a 'pay your money and you'll pass regardless' system that most would agree has both lessened the value of a license to operate, and significantly de-professionalised a once fairly professional industry.

Just because there are over fifteen thousand SIA CP licenses, does this mean there are over eleven thousand brilliant and brilliantly trained, professional CPOs? The philosophy and reasons for licenses should mean that yes, there should be, but most would say definitely not! There are more unprofessional and under-trained CPOs now than there ever has been.

By its very nature, this industry should be professional and should be elitist - as it is in most other countries around the world. Most security industry professionals would agree with me. Most wannabes would not! In most countries you would be laughed at if you said you were a professional protection officer after just having attended a 138 hour training course! Yet most CPOs have no other training whatsoever aside from their initial course. Most CPOs in the UK don't have any close quarter combat experience either (this is not martial arts or self-defense; close quarter combat skills enables you to disarm and disable a potential attacker and defend your client, which has a completely different skill-set than martial arts), and I have even met SIA qualified protection officers that cannot even drive... yes, there are qualified protection officers in the UK who don't even have a driver's licence!

The simple fact is that by over-commercialising close protection training courses - as the British Government has stupidly done - finding work in the industry is extremely difficult, because a standard SIA CP course does not guarantee professionalism as it should do. How can it, if virtually anyone can attend a course and pass? All the initial training (and an SIA license) now shows that you have a very (very!) basic understanding of CP operations and procedures. That's it. Oh, yes, it also shows that everyone has trained on roughly the same level as everyone else - 'roughly' being the operative word! Now, most companies just take your money, and your time, pass you whether you are good or not, give you an SIA badge and say *'off you go..!'* Many commercial training courses are now only interested in your money and have no intention at all in producing the very best CPOs they can, and of supporting them thereafter. And of course, very few training companies have any interest at all in helping newly trained CPOs towards their first CP contract - even if some training companies advertise that they do. This is a fact, and this is what commercialisation does to an industry in which commercialisation should never be a part of. However, saying all of that, there are still a few decent training companies left!

But why even mention these things? Because these are the real facts that every CPO should be aware of when looking for work, and it is exactly because of these things that finding work in the protection industry is not easy.

The aims of this publication therefore are to help the well-trained professional CPO find work, as well as to guide and support those who have just started their career in close protection. Because there IS work out there for the professional.

But first, how does one define professionalism in your career in protection? Actually, this can be quite difficult, but (as an example) if you stack shelves for a high-street retailer, with no previous security or related background and attended the cheapest CP course you could find just so you can get your SIA badge, and have no intention at all in doing any other training, then it's likely you are not too professional. It is also very likely that you will never ever get a job in CP anyway (thankfully!). And even if, with just a basic 138 hour SIA course under your belt but no other training, qualifications or experience, you still think you are good enough to get a job, then think again; with thousands of other licensed CPOs presuming exactly the same thing, it is also very unlikely your career will go anywhere.

It is true to say that most people currently working in close protection originate from a military or Forces background. In fact probably 85% of all *working* CPOs come from a Forces background. However, despite this fact and contrary to popular belief, you don't actually have to have a military career to enter and achieve success within the world of close protection (there are some brilliant CPOs that do not come from a military background). But, because you are mostly competing with former military and Forces personnel, you do need to be really driven and goal-oriented, and be willing to overcome the many obstacles that will be put in front of you, and of course not to give up! But it is possible and over the years I have personally known many non-military CPOs that have made a good living and have had a good career. There are not that many, and they tend to specialise, but they are out there, and these are the people who have invested in their own career by choosing the very best training courses (regardless of cost), have worked really hard, and have always strived for the very best and to be the very best. Most people don't however; most people give up, but those I know who haven't, have done really well.

Let me give you just one good example of how drive and determination can help you succeed in this industry. A few years ago I ran a *'How To Find Work as a Bodyguard'* seminar at a hotel just outside Windsor, UK. I had about twenty people turn up. Most of them went onto do do very little or nothing in CP after the course, as is usually the case! Most refused to follow my guidance and advice, and just wanted to do their own thing, for example blindly email their CV out to every security company under the sun in the vague hope that it might get picked up. This almost never works, yet surprisingly almost everyone does it! Why? I have no idea, but they do and they genuinely think this is an effective way to job hunt (and then they complain companies never reply to them!). Anyway, as the months and years passed, most of those people that had attended the seminar gave up trying to enter the world of close protection and went back to driving buses or stacking shelves or fixing cars, or whatever... About four or five had other security jobs, but did CP assignments now and then - perhaps one or two small jobs a year - mainly for the security companies that they were already working with. I heard a couple of people went on to work in Iraq for one or two tours, and then returned to the UK, couldn't find any other work and gave CP up too. As far as I know, only about two have been in the industry full-time since the *How To Find Work...* seminar. All the students who attended the seminar had a range of different backgrounds and experiences, but what did the two that remained in the business have that the others didn't ? Drive, determination, unwillingness to quit, and they listened to, and took the advise of others. I was honoured to meet up with one of them while I was in Bahrain a couple of years ago. He was working for the Saudi Arabian Oil Company (ARAMCO) at the time, and had to do the 'Bahrain run' to renew his monthly visa. I felt so proud when he said he had followed my advice and by doing so was still working in the protection industry many years later! Shortly after my seminar, he joined the Territorial Army (the UK's volunteer reservists) to get some military experience, attended the best CP training course he could find, and has been working full time in the CP industry almost ever since! He had been all over the world and, by his own admission, has a dream job. What was his career before he became a CPO? He was an accountant for a well-known London City bank! You would think that he was at such a disadvantage being a former banker, but he had more drive and determination that most, and has achieved exactly what he set out to achieve in his life. Absolutely brilliant and undeniably inspirational. We spent a day in Bahrain; I showed him around the island and then later that day he returned to Saudi. Recently I had an email from him; he is now Head of Security for a major UK educational institution and earning a very good salary. From his background he was perhaps at more of a disadvantage than most of the others attending the seminar, and yet none of the others have achieved anything like he has. Why? There is a good saying that I like to use:

"If you really want to change your life, you'll find a way. If you don't, you'll find excuses. "

It is easy in CP to find excuses for not working, but for those that don't depend upon excuses for their failings, it is possible to achieve.

And surprisingly you can do this too....

Of course I cannot guarantee that by following the advice in this publication, you will get a great CP job. But what I can guarantee is that by following at least some of the advice contained here, you should have a much better chance of finding a job. From setting up a professional CV, to approaching employers, networking - one of the most powerful tools of the trade – and setting up and working abroad, this manual is aimed at helping you to find positions... but it won't get you a job! That part is up to you; how you sell yourself at your interview and thereafter is in your hands alone, but this publication will try to guide you to that all-important interview!

Also incorporated within this manual is an updated *International Directory of Close Protection*. I had originally planned to publish this separately, but compiling such a directory is such a massive and continuous task and I have other commitment at present which is taking a lot of my time, so I have included an updated basic directory within this manual until such time as I can compile and publish one separately. Many of the contacts contained in the directory are extremely useful for CPOs looking for work, as well as to the CP community in general however, I completely understand I still have thousands and thousands more contacts to include, so make sure you do your own research and compile your own personal security directory of contacts.

I hope you find this manual useful. Read it carefully and use the information contained in it wisely; not everything will suit everybody. Print it out and underline or highlight key points, make notes and make a 'to do' list. Consider finding work the same as planing a CP operation; do your research, be systematic, be organised, find alternative routes, set yourself goals and above all achieve them!

Although this publication is primarily written for the UK market, many of the suggestions herein can be used by CPOs anywhere in the world, so don't let references to the SIA and the UK market put you off.

Lastly, you may agree with them or not, but unless stated otherwise, the thoughts and opinions in this manual are entirely my own. But please, if you have any tips and hints of your own on how to go about finding work in close protection, please do send them onto me as I am always extremely interested in new information and hearing about how others have entered this industry.

This publication will give you a start... but the rest is entirely up to you.

Stay safe!

HIGH THREAT CLOSE PROTECTION
By Richard Pendry

The outcome of the Iraq invasion in 2003 was an unparalleled need for close protection operators from companies that were providing security to U.S. Government officials in the aftermath of the Second Gulf War. Thousands of men and women flew into the war-torn country eager for a share of the American dollars that were being pumped in to the failing state, in an effort to keep it afloat. I know, because I was one of them.

This was the boom time with companies like Aegis, Control Risks, ArmorGroup, Olive, Erinys and the American big three; Triple Canopy, DynaCorps and the infamous Blackwater, all of which were making money hand-over-fist. Those who answered the call were paid well, with a thousand dollars a day being a common recompense for those prepared to risk their lives.

It was estimated that there were around 2,000 armed British operators in Iraq in 2007, with the overall number of civilian contractors helping the war effort running at around 120,000. The true figures will never be known as security companies - many of which register their interests in offshore tax havens such Virgin Islands - tend to shun publicity. The American figures show that 900 contractors were killed up to 2007. There are no official figures available for British casualties.

I left the army in the '80s and was content running my own business, the closest I got to the chaos and mayhem unfolding in the Middle East? The TV in my living room. I'd heard about the 'pop star' wages that security guys were getting for putting themselves in harm's way, but had no inclination whatsoever that I would soon be involved.

In 2005 I sold my company. With time on my hands I began looking for another business venture. I'd not kept in touch with my army mates and was completely out of the loop. But a chance meeting one day changed everything.

I bumped into a guy I knew from school. We'd joined the

army at around the same time, but had chosen different units. Our paths rarely crossed, but when they did we went for a beer and a catch-up. That day was one of those days. Over a couple of Heinekens, he told me that he'd had a call from an old army friend of his who was urgently looking for guys for Iraq. He'd signed up and was off the following week. As I drove home my mind was racing.

I told my wife of the conversation relaying it with excitement. She couldn't stop me talking about it. Eventually, after we'd finished a bottle of wine, she popped the question: "You've sold your business. Why don't you do it?" We'd been married for twenty years by then – that year was our 30th anniversary. She knew me inside and out. "I suppose I could," I replied trying to hide my excitement. "Maybe give it six months... a year tops." She put it down to a mid-life crisis. I was just fed up of the same-old, same-old. I wanted some excitement back in my life!

Now I'm an ex-Para. I didn't want to mention this earlier as not to discourage those of you who think that unless you have to have military background there is no chance that you can enter into the industry. True... it is easier if you have it, but it doesn't guarantee a right of passage. The industry is made up of an assortment of nationalities and backgrounds, including civilians. For instance, one of the characters in my debut novel Damascus Road (due for release in late 2015) is based on an amalgam of different civilian operators that I met on my way. He is a doorman from Watford who finds himself in Iraq, and gives a good account of himself when tested, even in the most sever of situations. So please read on, as this is not a tale for ex-squaddies by an ex-squaddie.

The key to a successful operation is preparation and planning. My objective was to get out to Iraq, so before my wife changed her mind, I needed a plan. I got in touch with some old Para mates of mine and quickly established that my friend had been really lucky. There were loads of people who wanted these highly paid jobs, and to stand any chance at getting a slot you needed a close protection course.

There were many courses out there providing close protection, but the two courses with the best reputations were South African run Ronin, and the British, Phoenix Close Protection. Both were expensive, the cost running into several thousand, but with a nothing ventured nothing gained attitude I decided for the latter, and wrote out the cheque.

I did a pistol course in Gibraltar for a week, and then the close protection course in Hereford, which was held in an old mansion house on the outskirts of the city. The association with the famous market town was a necessity rather than a cosmetic appendage - unlike so many companies nowadays who advertise a Hereford address in order to associate themselves with a Special Forces pedigree. No, it was a practicality because most of the people running the course lived in Hereford, as they were ex-SAS.

In total I spent four weeks under instruction with some of the best guys in the business; the wealth of knowledge and experience that the instructors were able to impart incredible. I was put under pressure – as were all my course mates - and pushed hard, all the while under the close eye of instructors who had spent a life time of training SAS soldiers. It was a pass or fail course, and just because you'd parted with thousands, didn't mean that you were getting a free ticket. On the final day we were called out one-by-one and given the good or bad news. Over ten percent failed. I didn't, and was allowed to go to the next step; the all-important interviews.

Now at this stage I want to take stock. One of the instructors - a wily ex-senior NCO with a lifetime in the Regiment - began to loosen up after a couple of bottles of Faustino V, and came out with this very pertinent quote. He said; 'There's a gold rush on, and Phoenix Close Protection is selling the shovels.' He hit the nail squarely on the head. To put this quote in context, we need to look at the industry prior to Iraq, 2003. The 'Circuit' was dominated by ex-military. The ex-SAS at the top of the tree with

Para's and Marines and various other cap badges lower down the pecking order. But if you weren't in the circle of trust, you stood very little chance of getting a break. Iraq changed all of that; It blew everything wide open. The ex-SAS guys started their own companies or took senior positions in existing ones. The effect was that everyone had moved up, allowing space in the bottom echelons for new operators to come in. But the SAS managers needed new recruits and they needed them well trained. Who did they go to for their new manpower? Phoenix Close Protection and the other companies out there run by ex-Special Forces mates. So, if you worked hard and past the course, you acquired the necessary skills and you got the all-important interview. You got to sit in front of the guy who was hiring. It was a well thought out process and an excellent business model. The moral to the story being that when you look for a course, make sure that the organisation will be able to point you in the right direction and provide you with the contacts. Because ladies and gentlemen, it's all about contacts, and the sooner you realise this the better chance you have at succeeding.

I landed in Baghdad in the summer of 2005. I remember the heat and a column of dark smoke rising up from the city ten miles away and thinking *shit, what the hell I have done?* When I arrived in the Greenzone I was briefed by one of the companies senior managers - an ex-Brit Mil brigadier - who informed me that I should make the most of my well paid salary as it wasn't going to last long, and not to have aspirations of a career in the security industry as this show – Iraq - would all be over pretty quick. Well... over ten years later how wrong was that pompous arse?

    I stayed in Iraq for well over two years, most of my time in the British controlled southern city of Basrah. I was at the tip of the spear. The documentaries on the news bulletins back home dispatching what was happening around me. They were hard, dangerous times, where some men died or suffered horrific injuries. But when I look back at them, I can't help but smile. It was an achievement. Some people climb mountains; I went to Iraq. It was where I learnt my trade.

The year 2015 sees my tenth year working in conflict and post conflict environments - to give Iraq and Afghanistan their more politically correct designations. I've moved on from being a 'bullet stopper,' my roles varying and diversifying as my experience has grown working for different clients. And we must of course remember that 'the client' is the key to the whole thing.

Working for a security company in close protection - or risk management to use the term that security companies have adopted to show their softer side - is all reliant on the client. The contracts differ from weeks and months, to years, with the organisations varying from aid and development companies to commercial entities; the one thing binding them together however is the requirement to do business in hostile environments.

The pot of gold at the end of the rainbow for most operators is to become the client, better conditions and far more money being the reward. I've know this happen quite often. The best example being the guys that were in Iraq when the oil companies moved in, many of whom were snapped up by large conglomerates desperate for the institutional knowledge that they possessed, gladly offering them a corporate position.

For the rest of the guys though its down to long rotations on wages that are getting lower and lower. I've recently heard of contracts in Iraq offering as little as $200 per day, with $250 in Afghanistan; your time-off spent in a small two-man room. Unfortunately the glory days are behind us, but there are still some good contracts out there, and of course it beats working for a living and if you play it right you don't pay tax. The result; you get to live like kings when your on leave.

So all-in-all what do I think of the last ten years? Quite simple; they've been amazing. I've done things that you can only read of in books, met incredible people, risked my life and am still here to tell the tale. Would I advise people to get involved? Again a resolving yes, but with the caveat that only those looking for adventure need apply!

Here's a couple of do's and don'ts and facts to get you started:

Do's
- Hostile environments normally involve guns so it would be a good idea to have some knowledge. Think about becoming a reserve soldier. There are also some really good pistol courses out there like the one I took in Gibraltar.
- Companies love it if you have 'in country' experience. If you cant get a slot, think about volunteering for an NGO. If you've got a foot in the door it usually opens.
- Do relevant courses. Close Protection is a must; First Aid is also compulsory. Languages are also very useful. Remember the cheaper is not always the better. Ask yourself; what will the course do for me?
- Think about a combined role, security and operations, logistics, HR, etc. Use your previous experience, adapt your CV. The more hats you can wear the better.
- Diversify your job search. Look on NGO websites and companies that are working in the area you have identified you want to work in.
- Be available at the drop of a hat.
- Network, network and network. Stay positive and learn to take rejection.

Don'ts
- Lie on your CV. You *will* get found out.
- Bad mouth the people or company that you work with.
- Cry off a job. If you've said your going to do it that's it you stick to your word.
- Let your team down. You want to be the good guy. Remember it's all about contacts. You want to be at the top of the list when they start making the calls. Good guys are always at the top.

Facts
- The Global War on Terror has not provided the expected results. The world is now a far more dangerous place than

prior to September 11, 2001. There are now far more countries that are considered 'hostile.'
- The security industry has grown incredibly since 2001 and shows no sign of slowing.

Good Luck!

***

Richard's book **Damascus Road, The Turning Point** *will be out shortly in paperback. "Mason, struggling after the loss of his family is forced to resign from the SAS. With nothing to loose he goes to Iraq to work for an old comrade in the cut-throat security industry. His team is forced on a suicidal mission; four are killed and two taken prisoner. Mason escapes helped by a mysterious Arab cult who live deep in the Basrah Marshes who are custodians of an ancient 'secret'. Blamed and discredited, he races against time to free his men, unaware that his journey to Damascus and down the great Euphrates, echoes' in the footsteps of the 'secret' and its guardian - a Crusading knight. The torment of the two warriors unfolds; their destinies entwined, echoing through time, as both search for redemption."*

BODY + GUARD?
By Timm Smith

Why on earth does the Security Industry Authority require a First Aid certificate for the licensing of Close Protection Officers, somebody should tell them we are bodyguards not first aiders! But wait a minute, we are body... guards, surely we need to know a little something about the body we are guarding or we would just be guards?

Is it not acceptable to just be a guard rather? Perhaps the answer to that question is to ask if we would be embarrassed if our Principal died on our shift from a medical ailment? Does it actually matter if the threat to his life came from inside himself or outside?

Ronin SA have always maintained that the answer to this dilemma is obvious; it matters if he dies on your watch – period!

This is why we have always strongly support the insight of the SIA on demanding medical competencies for any Close Protection Officer wishing to register. But have they gone far enough? Are the First Aid courses that are excepted by the SIA fit for purpose? We would submit that it depends where the work is for the First Aid at Work qualification to be fit for purpose. If it is an office within a country with a functional 999 system where politicians ask questions of the Honourable Minister of Health when Ambulance Trusts do not attend to 999 calls within 8 minutes, then perhaps yes the standard First Aid at Work, might do. But, what if it is a simple choking of the Principal at his local favourite eatery in central London, nothing sexy, he is choking, that's all? You try the first aid Hiemlich Manouvour which they taught you on first aid course and... nothing comes out! They go unconscious - they are now on borrowed time... 6 minutes to death and counting. Will the NHS Ambulance be there in time... maybe?

Is maybe good enough?

Was First Aid at Work good enough for a mere choking in

London?

We submit that it was not.

What is really needed is for the industry to realize that a HYBRID candidate (i.e. Tactician and Medic) with real ambulance time behind them, is the only true Body+Guard in existence and the rest are but part way to being one.

Ronin SA has trained 1600 graduates of which only 90 are hybrids. This outs an obvious flaw to our position; that is all good and well Ronin SA but where do we get these hybrids from?

The answer to that is that we need to change the way we train and recruit close protection officers or ensure that there is a HYBRID on every team with a covenant with G-d to not allow them to be the one that gets hurt when they are needed as The Medic by the Principal.

Clearly that is not possible as we are all sinners and G-d is fresh out of favours, so that leaves us with the inescapable truth that every team member should be a HYBRID tactician and medic.

A further reality is that after a tactical encounter there are numerous injured parties both team members and Principals, the "Medic" will be busy with the Principals and not the Team. Surely we have a duty to each other as Team members in that setting and should all have significant capacity to medically intervene on behalf of each other or indeed as medical force multipliers for the dedicated Medic.

There is a counter argument that soldiers are all trained as Team Medics and CMT 1 / 2 / 3 are good Medics. Whilst their trauma training may vary widely but be acceptable, what of the Principal is not injured via trauma but is having an Asthma attack / Anaphylaxis / Cerebro Vascular Accident / Hypoglycemic Coma etc etc... How many children and older unfit stressed patients have they seen?

The Solution

We need to change the way we train serious close protection officers and the Operational Companies in the industry must start by STOPPING:

- Their acceptance non-reality based training in the industry
- Their tick in the box mentality regarding CV's and verify credentials / courses
- Their "something like what reality requires" mediocrity for their Clients until the day it is outed by an real incident that "hopefully wont happen…"
- Their lack of understanding about who is really a medic (ambulance service veteran) and who is but a first aider who will not hold up their good name in the hour of need

Imagine the mileage you earn for a Operational company when you save a client via your medical skills - I have many times and if I am honest, about 7 out of 10 incidents in my career were medical and not tactical!

Our profession is what it is and we need too acknowledge its realities (Medical profile of the Principal) and be prepared for them in reality, as is our duty.

To train a Close Protection Operator as an Ambulance Technician or Paramedic can take years. So what do we do? Perhaps the Operational Companies should consider to START recruiting paramedics and ambulance technicians, and sending them for training as Close Protection Officers as it only takes 5 weeks to get a Hybrid operator that way!

We are doing our part by affording a 12% discount to Paramedics and Doctors who attend our course, to try to help the industry attain access to more HYBRIDS.

Conclusion

I am the messenger and have been for over 20 years, you are welcome to shoot us but as Malala says; "You cannot shoot our dream for the industry."

Please do not think you must come to Ronin SA to achieve your HYBRID status, go and do any ambulance based course anywhere in the world and touch patients and come of age as a true Bodyguard. If you have followed the logic of my rant today –

you are probably the kind of person we would love to meet at Ronin SA and welcome into our family of Hybrids.

Personal Safety & Self Defence

A PRACTICAL GUIDE TO AVOIDING AND DEALING WITH CONFLICT

TYRREL FRANCIS

OUT NOW....

TO JOIN OR NOT TO JOIN - THE BENEFITS OF CP ASSOCIATIONS
By Shaun West

My personal journey
When embarking upon a career within the Close Protection sector, I was extremely keen to be at the top of my profession by scouting out the best training courses available. I always chose quality over cost, when looking to undertake any form of professional development.

My mindset was that if I differentiated and marketed myself as a professional who invested in his future, then potential employers would recognize this. With this in mind, I aimed to build myself a solid foundation and started to create a professional portfolio displaying these new skills and qualifications.

For me, it was critical to carry out as much research as possible before entering the sector so that I would be coming 'fully armed.' The research that I carried out at pre-entry stage saved me thousands in cash, as well as countless precious man-hours.

Commit and make it your own
I would recommend that anyone embarking on a career in the industry carry out his or her own due diligence. Each individual's research should be different. Aspiring operators come from many different walks of life, with each candidate's background containing its own unique challenges. Some of the essentials that you'll need to be fully aware of are specific details such as entry criteria, the pros and cons of working in the security industry, salaries, level of competition, opportunities available, and so on.

Where to start
So the next consideration is, where can this research be carried out and where can you find the information that you need? There are many open source methods for accessing this valuable

knowledge that you will need in order to make an informed decision. First of all, it may sound obvious but Google is a fantastic resource and completely free. Then there are also channels such as LinkedIn and Facebook and, just as importantly though often under appreciated, is the need to seek out and speak with seasoned industry professionals. I gained so much knowledge just by speaking with people that I knew who were already established within the industry, as well as networking with others in the same position as myself in order to share experience, leads, and contacts. It didn't take me long before I realised that the CP sector is a very guarded and competitive industry. The more coveted work opportunities rarely get advertised and instead get shared within professional circles. It's therefore essential that you find a route into these networks, which usually means referrals and recommendations coming from the work you've already carried out.

What next…?
It quickly became apparent that I would need to expand my own personal and professional networks and so I set a plan in motion. I invested in having my CV professionally written, got some good quality business cards printed, created a personal website and spent the rest of my time attending networking events and joining various industry-specific associations and forums. Taking the time to present yourself in the most professional manner at this stage of your career may be your biggest and best investment. Reputations are quickly established in this industry and it is what holds the key to your future success.

I felt to only do one or two of the above mentioned things would be an injustice and would only be doing things half-hearted. So, in order to gain momentum and increase my network I made the decision to invest in my chosen career path and myself. This isn't just a financial commitment either. 'Fastballs' are the norm in close protection and operators who remain flexible and adaptable will progress quickest. I vowed to make myself available for every opportunity that would arise, often at the expense of family commitments and personal obligations.

Associations
Throughout it all, the single most important ingredient of my early success was the knowledge, support and opportunities that I gained through joining industry associations. I found that having other like-minded professionals to turn to, to be an invaluable resource and it certainly set me off on the right trajectory in my career. And so, a professional CP association holds space for professional growth and opportunities for the group. I was not afraid to ask questions if I was unsure of something, and I soaked up all advice given. In turn, I also held out my hand to help others whenever needed, this was all part of the group networking experience.

Since I entered the industry the landscape has changed greatly with the expansion of Facebook and LinkedIn so does that mean industry associations are no longer relevant? What you must first understand is that like anything in life, there are both good and bad associations and so it is up to the individual to research thoroughly and join only those which hold value and are specific to their needs.

Joining an established industry association opens you up to so many more opportunities - both personal and professional - and the more you become involved, the more benefits you can realise. An important question to ask yourself is: what benefits does this organization provide me? You should also ask yourself: what can I contribute to this organization that will, in turn, benefit me? If you're not sure how you will benefit from association membership, you should ask both the organisation and members from it.

Getting down to the details
So getting down to the nitty-gritty, what are the potential benefits to you for joining an industry specific association. Depending on the organization you select, you could benefit from any of the following:

- Credibility that comes with being a member of a respected

and recognized professional body.
- Increased employment opportunities.
- Eligibility for specialist CP insurance.
- Subscriptions to industry publications.
- Enrolment on developmental courses.
- Phone and email support.
- Invites to industry events, seminars, and workshops.
- Increased networking opportunities.
- Legal and financial advice.
- Professional development resources and tools.
- Discounts on industry services and products.
- Increased visibility, directory listings and promotion for your business or service.
- Introductions to a wider client base.
- Access to education, industry training courses, and certifications
- Ongoing support within a like-minded community.

The ultimate takeaway
The basic function of any association is to provide valuable information, appropriate/relevant training, and access to relevant materials that are not easily obtained from one source. Membership to industry specific organizations can be very valuable. Carefully consider whether the association you are looking at can offer you services or benefits that you are not able to access or achieve on your own at a comparable cost. When making a cost consideration, bear in mind that the cost of an annual subscription is usually far less than what can be earned from a single day's work. The return on investment for one day's work has been extremely valuable for me and I hope that it can be just the same for you as you embark upon your own journey towards career longevity.

Final thought: It is important to remember that when you join an industry association that you will get out of it what you put in - be prepared to get involved.

DECIDING ON HOW TO START YOUR CP CAREER
By Robin Barratt

Who has attended an SIA training course but have actually never yet done a day's CP work in their lives? How many months or years has it been since your course or, if you have worked, since your last operation? Who, when looking for a CP course, tried to find the cheapest course and quickest route possible to your SIA badge? Who researched their training provider and checked out all the credentials and qualifications of their instructors? Who doesn't intend to do any other training until they find at least some work to pay back their initial training costs? I could go on, but well, you get the picture...

Finding the right training course is a really, really important first step in your career in close protection. But it isn't an easy thing to do; train with the right company and you might be able to find work fairly quickly thereafter; train with the wrong company and you could easily have wasted thousands of pounds and a lot of time - it is likely that you will never get any work... ever! Train with the right company and your portfolio and CV starts to look good from the very beginning; train with the wrong company and your CV doesn't even get looked at! Train with the right company and you are considered a serious player who invests time and money in their career and wants to be the very best; train with the wrong company and, well you just get laughed at!

But how do you chose the right training course? Let's go back to an earlier question; *Who, when looking for a CP course, tried to find the cheapest course and quickest route to your SIA badge?* If you have this mindset when choosing a course, you are probably going to choose the wrong course and training provider! So before you start to choose a course, you need to consider your mindset! If your mindset is just to get a license, regardless of whether that license will get you any work or not, then choose any course by any provider and good luck! Because I can almost

99.9% guarantee you will never work in CP. However, if you are really determined to find the best course, how do you go about doing it?

The first and the most important thing to remember is that your initial close protection training should be just the first step of your training portfolio; further and on-going training is a must on the road to a really great career. Your compulsory 138 hours is just the very beginning; just a taster, if you like. After your course you will know a little bit about everything, but not a lot, so you have to consider taking other more specialised training shortly after your basic training depending upon your career path. And therefore, I strongly suggest that even at this early stage, you get to know what kind of close protection you are more interested in, and then try to choose a course training provider relevant to your career path. For example, if you do not intend to work outside of the UK, then initially investing in a course offering extensive firearms training will be a waste of money - employers operating in the UK will not need to know that you can field-strip an AK47 under constant mortar bombardment or double-clicking multiple targets while evacuating your principal! If you only want to work at events and concerts and with pop stars and celebrities, then select a specific training provider relevant to this particular sector of security and area of operations. There are a number of specialised well-known companies who only provide security for events, concerts etc., and so training with them will be far more beneficial to your chosen career path than choosing a general CP training course, and you can always upgrade your training to suit a new working environment and / or career path at a later date. Interested in female only security? Again there are a few female only operational companies that also offer CP training services. Interested in working in particular environments? Again, there are a few international companies that are licensed by the SIA, e.g. Ronin in South Africa. So think carefully about which area of close protection you are particularly interested in, and then do your research for specialised companies within these sectors that also provide CP training services. Don't just do a general CP course hoping to then decide where to take your career, because this is what thousands of people do and you'll be just the same as everyone else.

In my opinion, it is better to be a specialist than a 'jack of all trades.' I get loads of CVs sent to me every week, and when I look at someone's CV and they list loads of skills in different areas, I know that they probably have a good but basic understanding of many areas of CP, but a master of none. When I read a CV which lists training and experience in a few key skills and sectors, then I immediately understand they are a specialist. These are filed; because specialists are worth their weight in gold. The rest? Well... I get hundreds of CVs so why keep them? And I know that many big security companies feel the same; why keep average run-of-the-mill CVs when hundreds and hundreds come into our offices each and every week? It would be impossible to keep them all, and a complete waste of time reading them all too! So unless candidates state in their covering letter that they are a specialist, unfortunately most CVs go straight into the bin. Sorry, but this is a fact. So consider specialising at a very early stage.

Once you have decided on your career path and your particular speciality, after your initial SIA training course with the appropriate training provider, quickly invest in further, on-going training specific to that field, especially if you have limited operational experience.

It is an old story now, but every time I am asked about developing a training portfolio, I always refer back to a good friend who, over the course of two years, invested well over £10k on training; every spare penny he had, he put towards security and CP related training courses, and he travelled all over the UK - and abroad - developing his education. Because he was not originally from a military background and he found it very difficult to get established, he trained and trained; three or four courses a year for two years. He had no operational experience, he was not from a military background, however because of his huge training portfolio, he eventually secured a great position as a security driver with aristocracy in France, with a salary of £1000 a week, plus accommodation, expenses etc. He ended up staying in that job for over two years. His initial investment in training was paid back in just over two months. Do the maths!

He didn't make any excuses; he had a full-time job and worked bloody hard all hours, investing all the money he earned into his preferred profession as a CPO, and he made it. How many people have done this? Very few. How many people would do this? Very few too. It is easy, isn't it, to make excuses, but if you really want it, like my friend, you will do it.

IT'S NOT EASY BEING SECURITY
By Lawrence Snow

How a corporate security team can develop a brand and change perceptions and mindset of employees, customers, clients, and visitors.

It's a Hard Job
It's a hard job, employees think that you are only slowing them down in their daily routines; fire alarm drills, evacuation and shelter in place drills. Let's face it; your job is telling people what they can and cannot do. Asking for volunteers for fire wardens and searchers is sometimes like pulling teeth. It's not easy being security. Sometimes you are looked at being an annoyance (I can't open this door without security and they take forever!). Some may think you are a drain on the company bottom line.

So how do you change the mindset?
Be aware of your brand. Your brand is made up of employees having perceptions of your team, their personalities, likes and dislikes, how they react to an emergency or a simple request by an employee, how they dress, walk and talk. My guess is when someone mentions the accounting department it will probably elicit some type of feeling, an identity that you can relate to. Same goes for every department within your organization. You develop an image and mindset of what will happen. The same is true of security. When they hear the word security they have an image - good or bad.

How do you know?
How do you know if your security team has a bad brand? Ask! Create a survey and send to employees in either print or digital format via email. Analyze the answers. If what you read is negative and misunderstood you can influence what employees think of your department.

Develop your brand
Start with the foundation. Your brand is your DNA, your core. When it comes to establishing your brand, you should ask these important questions: Why do we do what we do? What are your values and beliefs? What's your department personality? Sometimes the mission and vision is crafted by the C-suite, even if it is, create your own style, personality, of what makes the security team. Now this probably won't be an easy task, but all of these pieces - what makes you tick, your personality, etc., - are absolutely imperative to defining or determining your brand. You'll need to set aside some time to figure this out. Off-site meetings are great way to clear the mind of the daily routine and brainstorm. Leverage corporate learning - in house or bring in an outside consultant, or attend e-learning sessions from a local college to help you figure out what a brand is and how you can develop yours. Once you have determined your brand, you will have to hone it so that you can effectively communicate it to peers, employees, clients, visitors, and other stakeholders. The reason is quite simple: No one knows who you are and what you are all about - until you succinctly tell them directly and indirectly.

Be your brand and influence others
Be proactive not reactive. Consistently exceed expectations; be professional, courteous, have a smile on your face, say good morning, dress professional; if you wear your own suits get them dry cleaned, put a little starch in your collar, dress for success, and put a little shine on your shoes. Be responsible for your own id, ego, and superego. Be your own brand and represent the brand of the security team. Security team members should have the right training. Of course the obvious; medical, weapons, etc., but just as important are these skills - like being an effective communicator - writing, grammar and speech courses.

Provide value and build trust. Market your brand
- Branding is the activity you perform to get your brand in

front of employees' eyes and ears. Branding is everything you do to let employees know about your brand. Here are a few tips to get you started:

- Create and deliver a monthly newsletter with content that can be used for employees at the office and at home.
- Create safety checklists; set up a few small casual info sessions for employees to come share what is on their mind - their ideas.
- Create your own digital platform - an intranet or internal website; this is your hub to bring employees eyes and ears.
- Create a weekly heads up email with content specific to what is going to affect or impact the employees - what is going on from security and community standpoint;
- Have "a meet the security team" meeting - more formal info session; Share your agenda - goals and strategies for employees
- Meet with the corporate marketing and communications team, leverage their resources like company-wide daily email, and leverage their know-how to share your brand visually and in print.
- Get some time in front of senior management meetings. (i.e. this is what we are working on, quarterly plans)
- Don't dictate. Include the employees in decision making issues- polls and surveys will give them a voice.

Good luck!

FINDING THE BEST CP TRAINING COURSES
By Robin Barratt

OK, so you have some idea of what you want to specialise in as a protection specialist, now how do you find the right course?

The first thing to do, of course, is to make sure the training company has the right accreditations and endorsements. If you intend to work in the UK and / or for a UK contractor then, at the time of writing this, you will need to attend an accredited SIA course. This may change in the near future but until it does the law still stands, and from the SIA website: *"An SIA licence is required if you undertake the licensable activities of a close protection operative and your services are supplied for the purposes of or in connection with any contract to a consumer. Unless your employer or company has been given an exemption under Section 4(4) of the Private Security Industry Act 2001, it is a criminal offence to undertake the licensable activities of a close protection operative without an SIA licence. An exemption is applicable only where the company in question has been granted approved contractor status by the SIA and the other conditions of Section 4(4) have also been met."* Therefore, don't waste money on a course that is not recognised or accredited, or go abroad to train with a non-accredited training provider, even if it might be a lot cheaper and even if you think you might never work in the UK! Things can - and frequently do - change and so spending a little extra on an accredited course now, might be of benefit in the future. At the time of writing this, to operate in the UK, or for a UK contractor abroad, you need one of these qualifications: Level 3 Certificate in Close Protection (Buckinghamshire New University), Level 3 Certificate in Close Protection (City & Guilds), Level 3 Certificate in Close Protection(Edexcel), Level 3 Certificate in Close Protection (HABC), Level 3 Certificate in Close Protection (IQ). Your training provider must be linked to one of these awarding bodies in order to offer close protection training. If in doubt, ask to see the training company's certification. Also, make sure your instructors are suitably qualified to instruct! In the UK, all instructors need to have an SIA recognised teaching qualification. All trainers in England, Wales and Northern Ireland delivering SIA licence-linked qualifications are required to hold the 'Preparing to Teach in the Lifelong Learning Sector' (PTLLS) or a recognised equivalent and/or higher level teaching qualification. All trainers in Scotland delivering SIA licence-linked qualifications are required to hold a teaching or training qualification at S/NVQ level 3 (or equivalent) that has been accredited by SQA/QCA or validated by HEI. Check with the training provider that they comply with the current SIA criteria. Some training providers have a number of instructors, but only a few of them have the approved teaching qualifications! Do not sign up for a course where the instructors are unqualified. Also, bizarrely instructors do not have to have any close protection experience in order to actually teach close protection, they just need the appropriate qualification to teach, so make sure you check them out too! Are they experienced? What is their background? Have they worked on the circuit as a Close Protection Officer recently? If so, when and where was their last operation? Have they been part of a team? Or Team Leader, or higher? Sadly over the years I have come across many, many instructors who have had very little or indeed no actual close protection experience, yet they were teaching close protection! True! There are also many instructors out there whose experience is from 10, 15 and in some cases 20 years ago. There is one well-known instructor in the North East of England in his late '50s who has done no actual close protection since his early thirties - he has been instructing for over twenty-five years with no recent, relevant operational experience! Ask yourself; is this how you really want to start your professional career?

There is a big, big difference between those instructing from a text book or from the past, and those instructing from actual recent operational experience. Make sure your instructors have recent experience in a variety of situations and arenas, as learning from someone with little or no field experience can be dangerous.

Ask the CP community via the industry forums and by networking about various training courses and training providers. There are many, many rubbish training companies (even if they do have SIA accreditation - sadly, like CPOs, SIA accreditation does not guarantee good training providers either), but of course there are many good training providers out there too. So if you have your mind set on a training provider, before you commit, ask other people if their training is both recognised and accepted within the close protection community, as well as by the major contractors? It is no good training with XYZ in so-and-so small town in the middle of no-where - even if they are SIA accredited - if none of the major contractors and employers know of, or are familiar with the company! Call major employers such as Control Risks, Hart, Minimal Risks, The Olive Group, Goose CP, Genric, Kroll, Drum, Aegis, etc., and ask which close protection training providers they most recognise and who, in their opinion, is worth training with. Many will, of course, tell you to train with them, as many contractors now offer their own close protection training courses, especially if they operate in high-risk regions worldwide. It makes sense that, from a contractors' point of view, it is much better to train your own employees thereby knowing what level they are at and exactly how they operate, rather than bringing in someone unknown who has had his / her training elsewhere or with an unknown company. I believe this is a good thing; if you are really good, you are then bound to be noticed for operations. When I ran my own courses in Wales and in Iceland during the '80s and '90s, I almost always used the CPOs I trained for my own operations. This makes sense for both the contractor and of course the individual.

If a contractor runs its own training course, before signing up to it, once again make sure you know their main areas of operation; find out what kind of work they do, and with what clients. For example, are they contracted to provide support to construction companies in Iraq or are they mainly known for celebrity protection? Perhaps, they work for insurance companies providing marine security. Most of this information is very easy to find and which also relates to the earlier advice I gave about deciding which area of protection you want to specialise in. Also, you need to know what kind of employees the contractor mainly uses, and what are the real chances of working with them after their close protection training course? For example, if a contractor operating mainly in war zones tells you it only employs former Special Forces, whilst a training course with them might be excellent, the chances of you finding work with them if you are not ex-SF would be extremely slim - even if you were the best student on that particular course! There are many high-end contractors that only employ former military personnel, so if you do not have a military background it is unlikely you will get any work with them - they just won't bring a non- military operator into a team of former military. Also, as a further example, there are contractors and security companies owned and managed by former paratroopers and who only employ people from the parachute regiment. I know of two such companies. So if you are not from the regiment, even if you train with them, you will not have any chance of getting work with them. But of course they might not tell you this as you sign up for their training, so do your research and find these things out before you train! No one can give you a guarantee of work, but if you're brilliant, top of the class and pass with flying colours, ask your training provider; will you get work with them? Ask! If you find asking is just too much trouble or even embarrassing, then find another career! Because if you are not dedicated, then you don't deserve to be successful, especially in this specific area of security. Go and guard a car-park instead.

Another important thing about finding the right CP training course; make sure you go and see the training school and meet the directors and instructors before you decide to train with them, or at the very latest, within seven days of placing your deposit or signing up on a course. You would not buy a car without seeing it first, so don't do it with something as potentially life-changing as your career (you will be amazed by how many people sign-up for a course without seeing the course provider). In the UK, it is a legal requirement to give everyone a cooling off period once a deposit is paid and / or contract signed so, if you are at all unhappy with the course provider, or if you find that the instructors are not accredited or cannot be verified or do not have relevant, recent operational experience, or indeed if no one is willing to meet and talk to you (they want to do everything via the telephone or email), then ask for your deposit back immediately! Cancel your contract and / or find somewhere else to train - there are plenty of training providers out there willing to meet and talk to you and show you around their facilities. Taking a day off work and losing £50 in petrol is much better than wasting £2k and a few weeks of your time on a course that will ultimately get you nowhere.

Also, get yourself physically and mentally prepared for the course and for your subsequent career in close protection. Sadly (and unbelievably), a high-level of fitness and experience in unarmed combat and / or self-defence are still not mandatory requirements for an SIA close protection course. It is true! But ask yourself whether you would employ someone overweight, unfit and unable to defend themselves or, much more importantly, their principal? Hundreds, if not thousands of people obtain their SIA licence in close protection without one shred of unarmed combat training and many are incredibly out of shape and extremely unfit too. I have personally witnessed an extremely overweight (fat!) person who could hardly manage to climb the second floor stairs to a class-room I was asked to lecture at, come out at the end of that CP course with a pass! He could hardly make the stairs, but got a British Government license as a bodyguard. This is deplorable if this wasn't so incredibly funny. Of course, he would never get a CP job anyway, but imagine him going into a foreign close protection team somewhere... he would be a laughing stock. There are no excuses and this should not be allowed and this is exactly why the British Government and the SIA have made a laughing stock of British bodyguards... but more on this later.

On another occasion I was asked to give a lecture in Manchester about the world of security and close protection in the Russian Federation. During the talk I asked whether the students felt they could 'look after themselves?' Everyone, without exception, put their hand up; all of them said they could. I then asked them which of them had intensive close-quarter unarmed combat training and had the skills to disarm and disable attackers with bottles, knives and guns, and who could probably teach these skills to others? One person - from a class of thirteen - put up *her* hand. Everyone had said they could 'look after themselves', yet no one had any training how to! If they didn't know how to disarm and disable opponents, how did they expect to look after their principal? I learned later that week that everyone on that particular course - yes everyone - had passed the course and all of them would be applying for their official Government approved SIA licence to look after the security and safety of someone else! Madness! How can some CPOs be so arrogant and self-important that they genuinely believe they can protect someone else without any self-defence or unarmed combat training whatsoever? Because it is not a legal requirement, which is the reason that most people would defend their arguments for not bothering to learn CQB; if you plan an operation properly, taking in every eventuality, then self-defence skills should never be needed. These idiots have evidently never been on an operation and have never experienced that, perhaps, things don't always go to plan! Important... if you are going to enter the world of protection, then learn to protect!

And lastly, if you're considering a career in close protection and are currently actively looking around for a decent training provider, please also be aware that there are still a few unscrupulous people preying on gullible 'wannabe' bodyguards. For example, I have heard of so-called training companies taking deposits on training courses (which are far cheaper than other courses), only to disappear with all the deposits and payments a few weeks before the course starts. Ten students paying £2k... worth the scam! Beware of on-line training and correspondence courses - all are now completely worthless in this industry and beware of false promises of work too; one company in the north of England (who, by the way, are still around and operating and have just been granted their SIA accreditation - unbelievable!) regularly guarantees every single student a real CP job within one month of training. What they won't tell you until after you have trained, is that the job is 'pro-bono' (which means you have to do it free), lasts for just a couple of hours and, more importantly, is a set-up job with the instructor's friend. Yes, this has been going on for years and everyone still falls for it.

So, if you are looking for a close protection training course, do your research and get as much information about the training company and its instructors as you can. Ask tons of questions and, most importantly, stick to referrals and recommendations from others in the industry (from those working and not from those who have not done any CP work in their lives) and don't train with a company just because they seem to be the cheapest or quickest... aim for the best!

SECURITY DRIVING AND SECURE TRANSPORTATION
By Tony Scotti

For some in the industry, especially those just entering the business; there is a misconception of what defines Security Driving, and in particular, the job description of a Security Driver. Security Driving is more than an act of driving a vehicle, it requires the skill and knowledge to move a principal from point A to point B in a safe and secure manner and in a variety of environments. In fact Security Driving is better called Secure Transportation, which includes an in-depth knowledge, and a measured level of skill to conduct route surveys; recognize and develop safe havens, alternate route plans, and develop emergency evacuation plans, along with advanced first-aid skills.

Recently Bodyguard and CP/EP Training doctrine suggests that Security Driving is a secondary skill, many times described as an, 'add-on', or training you may want to consider after you have been to an CP/EP training program. The facts are that it is not the training community that determines the skills sets necessary for employment, it is the job market. The most important members of the protection industry – the decision makers – those who have supplied protection based jobs for decades, have recognized that those who supply Secure Transportation are value-added members of the security team. Why does this market seek out those who have Secure Transportation skills? The simple answer is that most events that have shaped the industry and continue to be problematic have been and are vehicle-related.

In fact, the logic is inescapable; history and common sense dictate that security practitioners address the incidents that have the highest probability of occurrence, and for decades, every single credible study indicates that the overwhelming majority of security incidents involving corporate executives and high-profile individuals, including government and military, have occurred while the targeted individual was in or around their vehicle.

One of the most exhaustive studies to date, which was conducted by Gavin DeBecker, Tom Taylor and Jeff Marquart and published in the book *Just 2 Seconds,* indicates that 43% of all security incidents in which a specific individual was the target of an act meant to embarrass, harass or cause harm, occurred while the intended target was seated or riding in a vehicle. According to this study, which examined over 1,000 incidents worldwide, security-related risks are far more prevalent when the intended victim or target is in their vehicle, than at any other time or location. An analysis released on April 20, 2014 byIntelCenter, a private entity which provides intelligence to private sector and government clients, indicated that thus far in 2014 ,the majority of targeted kidnappings (34.15%) around the globe occurred while the intended target was driving. It's also worth noting that the subject matter experts at IntelCenter expect that trend to continue for the foreseeable future. Given the clearly defined risks associated with the executives travelling from point A to point B by car, it stands to reason that managing those risks should be a priority.

In conclusion:

1. The objective of personal security is to mitigate risk
2. The job market must address the incidents that have the highest probability of occurrence
3. The overwhelming majority of security incidents against the principal have occurred while the individual was in or around their vehicle
4. History has shown that the market seeks those with a skill-set that mitigate that risk.

So make sure that you enrol on a credible and professional Security Driver training program as part of your CP/EP training.

Who We Are

The International Security Driver Association (ISDA) was established to serve the Security Driving, Secure Transportation and Protective Services community.

The most important members of the industry – the decision makers, those who supply job opportunities have recognized that security driver/secure transportation professionals are value-added members of the security team.

The core of ISDA has 40 years of working and communicating with the Executive Protection/Protective Services market. There are few, if any, associations that represent this most important aspect of personal protection – ISDA fills that void.

What We Offer

- ISDA offers a precedent setting educational, mentorship, networking and marketing programs.
- **Education** – A major component of ISDA is to enhance the knowledge and education of the members through various online resources.
- **Networking** – Using the power of global networking ISDA will connect like-minded practitioners throughout the world.
- **Mentorship** – ISDA has created a Mentorship program.
- **Marketing** – ISDA will serve as the Brand Ambassadors for the Protective Services and Secure Transportation industry.
- **Career Center** – Members will have the opportunity to market their skills and for those in the private sector their services to over 20,000 security practitioners.

Certification

ISDA offers to its members that are eligible certification in Security Driving and Secure Transportation. ISDA is not like other associations - we do not offer training leading to a certification.

Membership requirements

There are no membership requirements to join, although we do recommend experience as a security driver, executive protection specialist or a security transportation provider to get the most out of the membership.

The cost of membership is $75.00 per year.

Learn more about ISDA visit our website: http://isdacenter.org.

FINDING WORK
By Robin Barratt

Without fail, I receive emails each and every week from people all over the world looking for work. Some emails don't have any message, just an attachment with their CV, others a brief note saying something like; *"please find attached my CV, contact me if I can be of assistance."* Most are not addressed to anyone in particular, just Dear Sir. Some have not been blind-copied, so therefore I can see that they have sent the same email to hundreds of others. Do people applying for work really think they will get a job like this? Sadly yes, many really do! But believe me, this is most definitely not a good way of finding work and I can guarantee that 99.99% of all these emails are never even looked at, let alone their CVs opened and read. Yet time and time again people continue to send these kinds of emails out to contractors and employees. There is work worldwide within the close protection industry but this is not the way to find it.

So what can you do to find work? If I had £1 for every time someone has said to me that there is no work in the close protection industry, I would be retired in a quiet little cottage overlooking the sea. In London alone, at any one time there are probably hundreds of CPOs working full-time and, over the course of a year, probably thousands on temporary contracts for concerts, private parties, special events, short-term assignments, visits, meetings, conferences etc. Globally there are more countries with the highest threat level (Cat. 5) than ever before. According to Hot Spots, Category 5 Threat Level means: *Locations can be affected by rampant violent crime, volatile situations of civil unrest, frequent terrorist extremist attacks and/or open military conflict.* There are many more countries with the second highest threat-level (Cat. 4). According to Hot Spots, Category 4 Threat Level means: *Incidents such as armed robbery, car-jacking, civil unrest, terrorism and/or extremist activity can occur frequently, and there is a greater risk that security issues could physically impact individuals and organizations.* In almost all these countries, almost every single foreign company or organisation employs security and security consultants. Also, countries like Bahrain for example, which has been on the news because of the troubles there, is classed in the third highest threat-level (Cat. 3). According to Hot Spots, Category 3 Threat Level means: *Incidents of violent crime, terrorism and/or extremist activity occur more frequently, but are still sporadic.* There are thousands of foreign companies working in all of these medium to high-risk arenas, and many of these companies employ security and protection; there are said to be tens of thousands of bodyguards operating in Iraq alone! Also,there is a Global Human Security Index detailing the countries where most people feel unsafe, with the Russian Federation deemed to be the most unsafe place in the world. These are the top fifty countries in the Index where people feel the most unsafe: Russian Federation, Somalia, Iraq, Israel, Georgia, Afghanistan, Korea, Sudan, United States of America, Colombia, Democratic Rep. of the Congo, Palestinian Authority, Sri Lanka, Thailand, Myanmar, Pakistan, Rwanda, Burundi, Dominican Republic, Chad, Zimbabwe, USA Virgin Islands, Philippines, Cuba, South Africa, Central African Republic, Brazil, Nigeria, Iran, Yemen, Belarus, Turkey, Ethiopia, Lebanon, Algeria, El Salvador, Kenya, Ukraine, Eritrea, Cote d'Ivoire, Uganda, India, Kazakhstan, Mexico, China, Venezuela, Saudi Arabia, Azerbaijan, Turkmenistan, Nepal, Egypt.

So, who says there is no work?

The only reason you cannot find work is that you have not spent enough time looking for work, or you just don't know how to.

Listen carefully... the phone does not start ringing just because you have spent £2000 on a training course and have your SIA badge! Yet bizarrely, most people spend every single penny they have on their basic training and then absolutely nothing thereafter on finding work. You can have the best product in the world, but it is useless if not a soul knows about it! And in my experience it is mainly the people that don't do anything proactive about finding work who are generally the ones that then complain time and time again that there is no work! Let me tell you once again... there are over fifteen thousand SIA CP licenses (in the UK alone, not to mention the tens of thousands around the world), so why should an employer pick you? What do you have, that over fifteen thousand others don't? I am being blunt and to the point, but you really must ask yourself these vital questions if you ever stand a chance of operating as a protection officer.

So what more can you do to find work in close protection? As I mentioned earlier, I believe one of the most important things you should do, is to decide very early in your career which environment and in which speciality you wish to work? You cannot do anything significant unless you make this fundamental decision. Do you want to work abroad or in the UK? If abroad, where? Define specific areas or countries and don't just say you can work anywhere, because quite simply; you cannot. So be specific; do you want to go to Iraq, Afghanistan, Liberia, Congo, Russia, Mexico, Eastern Europe, Asia? If you want to stay in the UK, or in western Europe, are you interested in corporate or celebrity protection? What about events, concerts, galas, opening nights, conferences, witness protection, residential security, corporate security, child protection, stalking consultancy etc.? However, keep in mind that if you only want to work in the UK, the chances of finding full-time work are a lot less - we just don't live in a high enough risk country (at the moment, anyway) for most people to employ full-time close protection.

By being more specific it then becomes a lot easier to target your potential client base and develop an appropriate marketing campaign; for example, corporate security in the Russian Federation or event security in Scotland. This makes your target market when applying for work a lot more defined and, more importantly, manageable, and if you have a good idea of where you want to work and in which environment and with whom, targeting employers within your defined sector becomes a little easier too. There are thousands of positions around the world and trying to apply for all of them is impossible and, as I have previously mentioned, blindly sending your CV off to everyone is a complete waste of time. You have to also look at yourself and be realistic about in which sector of CP you want to work in as well. For example, if you are 6'5", shaven head and built like a brick s**t-house, it is unlikely you will find a position looking after children or aristocracy, or within much of the corporate sector – celebrity protection is probably more of an option. But if you are short and skinny and unimposing, you probably won't get celebrity work, even if you are a combat specialist! If you are Arabic speaking it is unlikely you will find a position looking after Arabs on the Circuit in London, as they mainly want non-Arab speaking security so you don't overhear their conversations! Seriously! What they get up to away from their Muslim countries... well! If you are Indian, it is very unlikely you will get a job protecting a Pakistani client, if you are Jewish you won't be looking after Arabs, and visa versa. Even if you are white, it is unlikely you will be accepted in an all black security team either. So take a long hard look at yourself and then decide where you are going and what you are going to do. Do this first.

So, by looking at all of the above and analysing and assessing things in detail, you are now being more defined; who you are and what sector of security you are interested in, and where. Searching for work is now becoming a little easier!

Use the Internet extensively as a job-search resource, set aside at least an hour a day, every day, day-in, day-out and find out who employs whom, and in what environment. Let me tell you a little story, nothing to do with close protection and looking for work, but everything to do with motivating yourself to accomplish something. As many of you know, I am a writer and have written a number of books and manuals. And therefore I have many friends who are writers too. A few weeks ago I recently caught up with a writer friend who has just had his first book published; the first print-run of 10,000 copies sold out within two weeks! He woke up at 5 am every single day for over a year and wrote for three hours before going to his day job. Most of us would find excuses not to! He did not find any excuses, and was successful because of it. How many people reading this would wake up one hour earlier than usual in order to search the

Internet looking for work opportunities? I can guarantee... very few. It is easier not to, isn't it? And then, it is easier to complain about why you have not found a single day's work in close protection (or, for that matter, have changed your life in any other way).

Remember... you will only ever get out of it, what you put in!

As you are doing your research, start to make a list of employers and contractors within your defined areas of environment, speciality and expertise. As I mentioned, you cannot target all of the thousands and thousands of security companies in the UK alone, let alone worldwide, so narrow it down and concentrate on a small selection. If you make your daily target to find just five security companies worldwide (within your target market), times that by six days a week, you will of course have thirty possible employer's details. That's 120 a month! If you do this every day for six months, you will have 780 names, addresses and contact details of security companies operating within your specific area of interest. And, as you are getting data, check of course to see if they are advertising positions. If they are, and they suit your CV, then apply! But if their website says they are not accepting CVs, then don't be a prat and send them your CV anyway, it won't even get looked at, let alone read and you might even get blacklisted because you simply could not read the instructions on the website. This does happen! But instead keep a note of the company and the website for future reference and check back with them regularly.

However, saying that, many security companies just do not advertise their positions, so sending your CV either via email or snail-mail might possibly work if - and only if - you call them first and ask if they are recruiting. Ask for the name of the person in charge of recruitment and try to speak to them directly, if you can. Ask if they are recruiting and if so, can you send them your CV? If they say no, then don't send it and don't try to talk them into receiving it, as for sure it will go in the bin and again you might get blacklisted! I remember once someone doing just this, he called me and asked if I had any positions. I didn't. He asked if

I was accepting CVs anyway, I wasn't, but a few hours later he emailed it to me anyway! Did I waste my time reading through it, when I get hundreds of CVs sent to me? Of course not. Why would I waste my time reading his CV for no reason at all? as I had no positions and wasn't recruiting and I told him this. It makes no sense. So if employers are not recruiting, be polite, make friends with them and arrange to call them back at another time. But if their website says that phone enquiries are not welcome, then don't call them either! Remember, wasting the time of a recruitment officer or an HR department of a big security company does not bode well for your future employment prospects.

It is important to have a notebook and make a systematic structure of who you have called, who to call back on, where and who you have sent your CV and who has replied. Get names and direct telephone numbers if at all possible, and once you have agreed to send your CV to a recruitment officer, always follow it up with a telephone call a week or so later. Ask them if they've received it, if they have managed to read it and if not, ask when would be a good time to call them back, and make sure you call back! And if you are told you are not suitable, try to find out why. This is important, as if you get knocked back time and time again because of the same reason, you will want to be doing something to change this! Don't be overbearing and don't harass them, but if you can, try to develop an ongoing rapport with HR, it really does work. For example, one time I had 70 CVs sent to me for a five-man team I needed, but I did tend to look more closely at CVs sent from the people who had called me and whom I had spoken to. It is natural, and if you don't have the guts to pick up the telephone and speak to people directly, then you definitely don't have the guts to be in this industry!

Also, of course, make sure your CV is perfect – no mistakes and no bullshit. More on CVs later...

In close protection, because of the nature of the job and its tasks and the close dependence on the team, CPOs naturally tend to work with people they know and trust. So, effective networking is still a great resource, as many positions are filled not by adverts on job boards or websites, but via word of mouth and from referrals and recommendations. And so, it is vitally important to make contact with as many people in the industry as you possibly can, as one of them might just one day give you that vital 'heads up' on a great position. More on networking later too...

Join close protection forums as they can also be a good source of information, even if some of the notices and threads are very unprofessional, extremely arrogant, and occasionally political (you will also notice how unprofessional threads usually come from people out of work!). However, there is still a lot of great information to be had via the forums. But don't forget that when a position is posted on the forums, it is viewed by literally thousands of people and personally, I have not heard of too many being filled just by posting them on the forums.

I do believe that everyone in this industry should work together, because as a group you can achieve so much more than you could as an individual, but sadly for some bizarre reason most CP forums in the UK compete with each other and guard their membership database mercilessly. Many won't even list conferences, seminars, meetings or talks run by other forums or organisations which could be extremely beneficial for CPOs. For example, I tried to post details of an annual close protection symposium I was trying to set up for the industry on one well-known CP board, and even though it would be of immense benefit to CPOs across the UK and beyond, they took it down (and banned me) because it wasn't that particular forum that was organising it and therefore saw it as competition to them. Idiots! So keep in mind that forums can be very biased and will only post what they want to show or what they are getting paid to show. It is pathetic and unnecessary - we are all in this business together and trying to make a living doing what we love, and the more we can work together the better this industry will be. But hey, that's just my opinion...

And so, if you join a forum, remain professional at all times and do not get involved in petty arguments and do not slag anyone else down, or criticize anyone. Don't forget, what you write on a forum stays on a forum! What do you think a contractor or employer (or client!) will think of you if they came across your vengeful posts! So think carefully before you write or post anything!

As well as joining the forums, you must also dedicate a few hundred pounds a year to joining some good security and protection related associations and professional security CV databases, and subscribing to security magazines, as well as attending as many network events as you can. These are not only really great ways of developing your knowledge base, but can also give you some great information on contracting, company take-overs, tendering, etc., which could help in your search for work. If you read that a security company has just won a bid to provide security somewhere, what is the first thing you are going to do? Yes, contact them! But you do need to know about these things, so get the magazines and join the groups! As one CPO said to me recently; *"Apart from as much free networking as I can do, I have also dedicated three hundred pounds a year to job-search services, subscribing to security magazines and to joining security associations. Sure, some money will be wasted but some won't, and hopefully what works will more than compensate for what doesn't."* He also said to me; *"If I only get two day's work a year, then it has paid for itself, but you just don't know what is around the corner and who you might one day talk to."* What a great attitude!

A FEMALE CPOS JOURNEY INTO THE INDUSTRY
By El Mitropoulou

After nine years in the army, El went on to train as a bodyguard. Completing her close protection and firearms training in Slovakia, and her medical training in Guatemala, Central America, El spent two years on protection duty in Afghanistan and is currently working in Iraq; two of the most hostile regions in the world.

This is her story...

As my very Welsh name suggests, I was born in January 1985, Neath, South Wales. Well... perhaps not! Born to an English mother and Greek father, whose summer romance blossomed into marriage, two daughters and, as happens with most modern marriages, an early divorce.

My mum decided to give birth to me in Wales as her family (my grandparents) lived there and she wanted their support. And I guess she also thought that the health care system was better in the UK. Another sneaky reason was in case I was a boy; I would then be exempt from the mandatory military service for men in Greece. So I was born in Wales and, a few months after, we moved back to Greece.

My mother was a primary school English teacher and brought myself and my sister up on her own in a foreign country, with no help whatsoever from my bar-tender, alcoholic, ill-tempered father. He left when I was six and, even at that early age, I was glad to see the back of him.

My mother gave my sister Danae and me the happiest childhood we could have asked for, I don't know how she managed with money being so tight, but she made our childhood an extremely happy one. Always educating us, but in a fun and relaxed manner, never forcing views or opinions on us and, from a very young age, letting us be very free and independent. She was never pushy, she just let us find our own paths in life.

From what I'm told, I was a serious child. I enjoyed reading, drawing and was happy in my own company. My mother says I was an easy child to look after, as long as I had books, crayons and later on, Lego, I was happy.

Growing up abroad had its benefits; I grew up bilingual and in a multicultural society in Athens. Although my family had little money, we were lucky enough to have a property in an affluent suburb where many expats resided. That exposure to all different nationalities definitely shaped my character in a positive way.

My schooling was a mix of the Greek education system and the British. More so the Greek, as that's where I eventually graduated from high school in 2002.

I had great friends throughout my school years in Athens, and still to this day speak to them and meet up with them when time allows. Being a January baby, I was one of the youngest in my class, so initially I was smaller than the other kids - but that was never a problem as I befriended people easily, and bullying didn't seem to exist back then. I was a popular student and involved myself in student politics throughout my schooling, and in high school I was voted Class President and represented the school in the European Youth Parliament.

I was, without putting in much effort, an average student. My favourite subjects by far were History and English. I was abysmal at Maths and struggled with Greek and Ancient Greek - I've heard it said that a person can only think in one language and I think in English, so going to a Greek school was sometimes a struggle as I'd often have to translate things in my head between the two different languages.

As a teenager I was most definitely a little rebellious and playing truant in a Greek school is rather easy, as you're allowed a fair few unexplained absences per year. Also, in Greece, kids don't wear school uniform so that helped with my truancy escapades. However, I wasn't a trouble-maker or into drugs - there was a massive amount of kids that were into both those things - and I think I was liked by most of my teachers.

I believe I lacked direction though, with my mother working all hours God sent and not really being able to keep tabs on me, combined with her not imposing any strict rules and punishment; I was allowed to just be, which was great as a kid, but honestly I had no idea what I wanted to do in the future and no clear path.

I did work though, to earn myself some extra money. My very first job was a summer job working in a bar/café in Kifissia, Athens. I was employed illegally as I was only fifteen at the time, and I continued to work there in the summer months and on weekends up until I finished school. It was a popular little rock bar, where a young crowd would take advantage of the very lax rules regarding selling alcohol to minors. I remember the police would turn up every so often, after complaints about the noise, and I and the other under-age workers would run up to the rooftop and hide out there until they'd gone. The boss was quite an old guy who everyone referred to as 'Pappou' (Granddad in Greek). He was a nice guy but seldom paid on time, and often underpaid or cut wages as and when he felt like it. Still it was a fun crowd to work with and I enjoyed the music.

My second job was a job my mother arranged for me after my last year at school. Being an English teacher she was often asked to teach kids privately, but she had a full schedule that summer and so passed the opportunity on to me. Having no teaching qualifications and being only seventeen, I did however possess an English accent and my mum was a respected teacher, and apparently that was enough to get me the job. And so I spent that summer teaching a little Greek boy English and living at the hotel where he spent his summer holidays. It wasn't especially taxing, I was just expected to spend about four hours a day with him, playing games and talking to him in English. Still I couldn't stand it; the boy was spoilt rotten by his super-rich, mostly absent parents, and totally mollycoddled by his overbearing grandmother. But what the job did teach me was new-found respect for the work my mum did. I don't think I realised up until then how patient and skilful she was in dealing with children.

I finished school in 2002, 1st Lyceum of Kifissia. I left

with fifteen GCSEs (Greek equivalent of), just what was required in order to finish high school back then and gain entry into Greek University. I never actually bothered to send my results to the University selection board, I have a vague recollection of my mum sending them on my behalf, but I had no intention of furthering my education in Greece. That autumn it had been decided that I should move back to the UK. My grandparents (obviously sensing my lack of direction) had asked if I should like to move in with them after the summer and explore my options in Wales.

And so, after that last summer in Greece, I headed back to Wales, to my grandparents' house, not really knowing what the future held for me. It was my grandfather that suggested to me that I could look into joining the Armed Forces. I went to the recruitment office in Swansea to see what they had to say, and obviously liked what they said because a short while later I ended up joining the army, Royal Corps of Signals, as a Radio Systems Operator, and enjoyed a nine year long career, from 2003 to 2012, finishing at the rank of Corporal. I served in UK, Germany and Northern Ireland and deployed to Iraq once and Afghanistan twice. I also spent time in the Falkland Islands, Ascension Islands, Nepal, Czech Republic and Poland.

The most difficult time of my life was the period leading up to and me leaving the army. Up until late 2010, I never even thought of leaving, I was doing well, getting promoted and had just joined a prestigious Signals Unit. I wanted to stay and follow the Yeoman of Signals career path and serve for twenty-two years. But an unfortunate accident changed my world; I broke my ankle during my promotion course. I made a full and quick recovery, was then deployed to Afghanistan and on my return from operations, demoted for failing to comply with a new army policy to complete the promotion course within the year - despite the fact that I had to deploy to Afghanistan and my then Unit's role there was critical. I was told I had to go, course or no course. Also the policy was never really publicised or implemented properly; I guess I, like many others, got caught up in this bureaucratically silly situation. I appealed the decision to demote me, after all I felt I had proven my worth on real-time operations in Afghanistan. After a long and bitter battle I won, my rank was reinstated and an apology issued. But it was too late, I had become so disgusted and disillusioned with the way the army had treated me post-accident, I couldn't bear to stay in any longer. I felt the way they had behaved was an undeserved slap in the face and made a mockery of my exemplary Service for all those years of my youth.

I don't regret my time spent in the army though, it was a life experience that I - for the most part anyway - enjoyed and I was proud to serve my country. Although half-Greek by birth and spending my childhood in Athens, I have always considered myself more British than Greek. That does not mean that I don't also acknowledge and respect my Greek heritage. The skills and life lessons I learned whilst serving cannot be learned in what us ex-soldiers like to call civvy street, and the friends you make along the way are friends for life.

An army career in communications would have probably seen me safely into a civilian communications job but - and with no disrespect to the people that work in that industry - I just didn't want to slip into the civilian equivalent of my previous job. I wanted something new and, to be perfectly honest, I needed some direction. Fortunately for me I will always be grateful to my Resettlement Officer for suggesting close protection, something I'd never even thought of, let alone considered as a new career path. Admittedly it sounded quite interesting, and the more I looked into it, the more I thought this was something I would enjoy; it involved adventure, travel, diversity and, let's be honest, the prospect of a significant pay increase.

The more research I did, the more sold I was on the idea - but I knew nothing of the security industry and how it operated. Would I actually be employable? Again, as luck would have it, I was put in touch with an individual in the industry who took the time to meet up with me and discuss everything. And by everything, I mean everything; the poor man must have felt he was being interviewed on *Question Time*. After our lengthy informative conversation my findings were that yes, there were jobs going, and even more so for females who were in short supply on the circuit (the term used for bodyguard employment).

Wanting the ability to be able to be employed in executive close protection and hostile close protection, I elected to complete my close protection course with a training provider that included a firearms package, as well as the other modules required for completion of the Edexcel BTEC Level 3 Certificate in Close Protection. I really enjoyed the training and, as with most courses I had completed whilst in the Armed Forces, I found myself being the only woman on the course. A fact that has never fazed me, in fact I believe that being a minority in a group can make you strive to better succeed in all aspects of life.

It soon became apparent that close protection was not about running around guns blazing and pretending to be Rambo - although aggression when required is imperative to the job. Most of the training concentrated on the ability to plan, organisational skills, and building a sound professional rapport with the client/principal seemed to be the key to success.

The firearms training part of the course was especially educating as, during my time in the military, I was generally only exposed to a few types of weapons, but whilst firearm training in Slovakia as part of the bodyguarding course, I had exposure to a multitude of firearms which was very beneficial and of course extremely confidence building.

Conflict management was also taught; being able to defuse a situation without having to resort to the use of force is an attribute every good close protection officer should possess. However, some unarmed combat skills were taught and the importance of maintaining a good level of fitness was stressed to all students.

Medical training to at least First Responder standard seems to be an industry prerequisite in securing a good security job these days, and rightly so. Whether you find yourself working in a European capital or the Middle East, the ability to be able to provide first aid to the principal, yourself and, if the situation allows, your colleagues is invaluable. I chose to do an Emergency Medical Technician (Basic) course, along with a First Person on

Scene (Intermediate) course in Guatemala, mainly because of the ambulance attachment during the last five days on the course and, quite frankly, because I quite fancied visiting Central America. I won't lie, all this training cost a considerable amount of money but my goal was to make myself as employable as possible; it was a gamble that I hoped would pay off.

The Olympic Games 2012 in London created a backlog of SIA licences awaiting approval and sadly my Front-line Close Protection Officer licence was also stuck somewhere in the system. It took considerably longer than I thought to obtain my licence. In the interim, I did what I was advised to do on my close protection course - I networked. I sent my CV out to every security company I could think of. A good tool for this was using the list of companies that had signed the ICOC (International Code of Conduct) for Private Security Service Providers.

I created an online professional networking profile and attempted to connect with as many individuals as possible in the industry. I also obtained a second passport and kept up-to-date with current affairs, after all I was hoping to find work anywhere.

It was a long and frustrating wait, without an SIA licence (in the UK, a Security Industry Authority licence is required to work in close protection), most companies would not even look at my CV, and there were times when I thought I had perhaps made a major mistake in my new career selection.

Finally my SIA licence did arrive; I could finally cross out *awaiting licensing* from my CV and online profiles, and replace it with a licence number. This did improve my chances of the company HR actually looking at my CV, but with no previous close protection experience it was still very difficult to get that 'foot in the door' moment.

My opportunity came unexpectedly one day when I received a message on a professional networking site asking me whether I'd be interested in working in Kabul on a diplomatic contract. Safe to say I was interested! After a successful interview in London, numerous background and vetting checks, a job offer was made. The sense of relief I felt was enormous; this was my break and my chance to prove I could do the job I'd been trained to do for real.

Deploying as a contractor was a significantly different experience to my previous deployments in the military, where everything is pretty much organised for you and all you have to do is turn up. Again, a lot of research was required whilst waiting for a visa and a deployment date, and my days were spent looking for as much information on the country, company, as well as the contract I was to be employed on. Contacting other soon-to-be-colleagues was invaluable too, all of whom were very helpful and happy to discuss things with me - from what to take with me, to what to expect on my induction week, fitness tests, weapon handling and ranges. Simple information like for instance; Dari and not Pashto is the predominant language used in northern Afghanistan, and that Kabul rather unlike the south of Afghanistan, actually experiences harsh and long winters - also very useful to know.

I subscribed to every online newspaper, blog and weather site pertaining to Kabul and Afghanistan, and daily followed all the posts. Although during my military career I had been deployed to Afghanistan twice previously, I had never spent any time in Kabul - this was going to be an exciting and challenging time.

Having spent just under two years in Kabul as a contractor, on both diplomatic and commercial contracts, I can safely say I made it! I have managed to achieve my goal and get out there and work as a close protection officer in one of the most hostile environments in the world today.

The experience I've gained so far has been a real education; from remembering, nervously, heading out on my first driver-training on the mean streets of Kabul, to now confidently navigating around the city and the infamous Kabul traffic without hesitation - not to say I haven't had the odd bump or two though; from looking at a spot-map of the city, thinking how on earth am I going to remember all these locations, to now conducting recces (reconnaissance) on new locations for clients to visit; from covert jobs wearing local dress and hijab, to full scale overt sporting chest rig and molle belt, and even on occasion having to wear the dreaded fashion faux pas but entirely practical fishing-jacket. Jobs that take me all over the city, to ministries, embassies and NGOs and venues that include restaurants, private residences and public spaces, providing a true challenge in terms of keeping clients safe. And provincial visits to cities across Afghanistan; Mazare-Sharif and Herat, requiring advance party reconnaissance of locations, and coming to terms with even more city idiosyncrasies and cultural differences, and interaction with the local population and law enforcement. And in a city living under the constant threat of terrorist violence, comes with the risk of losing some good friends, may they rest in peace.

Often I get asked; what's it like being a woman operating out there? Generally it's fine. Of course, there are differences between male and female close protection officers, but there are also many differences between individual close protection officers. I can only speak for myself, and my experiences working out in Kabul have been, on the whole, good ones. Acceptance by male colleagues is very important; initially you do have to prove you can bring something to the team, but once that's taken care of, and as long as you don't prance around like an airhead combat Barbie, you start to earn their respect. Having a woman on a close protection team has many advantages too - the ones I noticed whilst operating in Kabul were mainly being able to take a weapon into venues where perhaps male colleagues wouldn't be allowed to bring one in - due to the reluctance and hesitation of Afghan men to interact with foreign women and the considerable lack of Afghan female searchers at venues. Again because of the predominately male Afghan society, defusing potentially tricky situations or negotiating check points - as a foreign woman - is easy, quite simply because the local men don't really know how to react to you and they are most of the time unsure of who you are - the concept of female close protection officers is still simply quite alien to them.

An increase in the number of women employed in the embassies, consulates and NGOs has created a larger female client base which, in turn, has created a larger need for women CPOs in support of them. However, the whole time I was operating in Kabul I met no more than ten other women close protection officers operating out there, women of a variety of nationalities, most with previous military or police experience, some with none. Young and more mature women, I even met a grandmother. But what struck me was the distinct lack of number of us. In an industry where reputation is key to future employment, with such few numbers, if you mess up or are unprofessional in any way this will follow you and stick with you for the rest of your career. Being professional, courteous and maintaining good relations with bosses and colleagues goes a long way.

Also CPD (Continuing Professional Development) is something to keep on top of, to improve employment prospects in the future - there's always something new to learn.

I am fully aware that the work I'm doing at the moment has an expiry date. Close protection officers must be young, fit and healthy in order to be able to operate to the best of their ability and remain at the top of their game. I've recently turned thirty and, realistically, I could probably continue to do this job for another fifteen more years, but I'm already thinking about the future and preparing for it, mainly by furthering my education. I wish to remain in the field of security and hope to start a degree in Security Consultancy this coming September. A degree, combined with the on-the-ground experience I'm gaining at the moment, should hopefully put me in good stead for a change to management positions in the future. That's the dream anyway! I know how quick things can change in this industry so I always keep this in mind. And if, for whatever reason, I'm unable to continue doing my job, I know that I'm not work-shy and I'll just pick myself up and try something new, perhaps in the travel or hospitality industry, which are also areas of particular interest to me. My immediate future plans also include more travel - a true passion of mine - combined with volunteer work; I'd like to give back to the world and less fortunate, especially the young. I'm considering gaining my TEFL (Teaching English as Foreign Language) qualification in order to be able to use my spare time teaching English to impoverished areas abroad.

To quote a line I heard in the movie *My Big Fat Greek Wedding*: "Don't let your past dictate who you are, but let it be part of who you will become." However much I struggled or didn't understand events of my past, the culmination of events and experiences have made me who I am today, so considering that, for the most part, I enjoy my life and like who I am, I can't think of a singularity I would like to change. I would however make a more conscious effort to listen to people who matter and try to be kinder to all.

I try not to think too far ahead though, far enough to have a plan but thinking too far into the future scares me! All I know is that with the job I do, I have to make sure I make the most of my time off, to create memories with people I love and enjoy life!

***

Extract from the book **Britain's Toughest Women - Some of the toughest women bodyguards, bouncers, bodybuilders, boxers, martial artists and MMA fighters in the UK**. *Available now as a paperback: ISBN: 978-1508941262 and Kindle: ASIN: B00WA7OT0S*

INTERNATIONAL CONSULTANCY
By Robin Barratt

One brave option to almost certainly find work, and be one of just a very few protection specialists operating within a specific environment, is to start your own security consultancy company specialising in a specific high-risk part of the world. In other words; making you own market! For example, if you specialise in close protection and supply security services to foreign companies and organisations trading and operating in the Democratic Republic of Congo, and you market this carefully within that country, it should not take you very long to develop a good network of clients who would most certainly use you and your services because, quite simply, there would not be many other people that do! I did this in Moscow, Russia in the mid '90s and was one of just a handful of British ex-pats permanently living in Moscow at the time who were recognised for providing close protection and security services. And because of this, it didn't take me very long to develop a network of clients; British clients based there, British clients visiting and a few foreign (and some Russian) clients wanting British led security services. Us Brits may have a bad reputation in many things abroad, but wherever you go in the world, we still do have a very good reputation for providing some of the very best security services. Of course, you have to choose a country that is rated as non-peaceful and medium to high-risk; being a bodyguard in Iceland, for example, where the risk of assassination, kidnapping and extortion is negligible and is classed as one of the most peaceful nations in the world (apparently, but its capital Reykjavik on a Saturday evening is not for the faint-hearted!), will not do too much for your close protection career!

Aside from obvious war-zone countries like Afghanistan and Iraq, there are probably over a hundred other countries where peace is fragile and where CPOs are routinely deployed to look after the rich, famous, wealthy and important. One of biggest employers of bodyguards within the civilian environment is the USA, which is ranked 9th lowest in a peace index, below Sudan and above Columbia. Hard to believe but true - people really do feel safer in Sudan than they do in the USA and, according to the FBI, there is an average of 6.7 kidnappings and 5.5 murders for every 100,000 people in the United States – one of the highest in the world. The Russian Federation is likely to be the second biggest employer of BGs as it is currently ranked lowest in the world for peace, above Iraq and Afghanistan! Yes, according to a recent Security Poll, people also feel safer in Iraq, Afghanistan and Somalia than they do in Russia; almost every big business in Russia has teams of guards protecting its senior management.

As I have said, the really great thing about setting up abroad is that you will be one of a very, very few; which itself makes you much more employable. When I was in Russia, there were not many Brits permanently living in Moscow providing security and protection services (in fact, there still aren't!), and there are definitely not many in Congo or Sudan! In the UK if you have an SIA license you are currently one of over fifteen thousand Close Protection license holders also looking for work. In Moscow, as a foreigner, you may be one of perhaps ten. In Congo one of perhaps...one or two, so suddenly you become a very big fish in a tiny pond. But it takes a completely different mindset to give up the relative calm and familiarity of living and working in the UK in order to start providing security and protection services in some god-forsaken part of the world. It isn't for the faint-hearted or easily intimidated, and it isn't easy either. I remember talking about these options to one CPO I met a couple of years ago. When I suggested he consider setting up in a dangerous, high-risk part of the world, he quite literally said, *"God no, couldn't do that, far too dangerous!"* Seriously?!? He never did get any work and last time I heard he was a taxi driver in Manchester. But if you are that way inclined, and have no ties and a little money behind you, then perhaps setting up abroad could be a really great way of establishing yourself as a country specialist. In the right environment it wouldn't take you too long to get established and start earning a very good salary. However, you can't just pack your bags and off you go; like every operation you have to plan things very carefully, and do a ton of research, check visa and immigration requirements, find accommodation, do a couple of recce' trips and make as many contacts as you can before moving out. There are lots of obstacles and hurdles to overcome, and it might not be easy (if it was, everyone would be doing it, but in fact few ever do), and anyway, who wants easy? But I did it in Moscow, and if I can do it, anyone can. I have come across many, many people living and working as protection specialists in all sorts of places around the world, many even on tourist visas! (It's a bummer if you get caught working on a tourist visa though, and would probably result in deportation, but for many this is certainly one way of settling in and getting established until able to set themselves up legally). Someone British doing business in Moscow would almost always trust a fellow Brit for their security and safety, rather than to a Russian or Russian only security company and when I lived and worked in Moscow I met a few other Brits who also operated as security consultants, and none regretted it, even for a minute, and most were almost continually employed and had earned a great deal of money. Actually, this goes for almost every nationality anywhere in the world; rightly or wrongly we almost always trust our own in foreign and strange environments.

So how do start such an adventure? One of the first things to do when arriving in a new country is to contact your Embassy, introduce yourself and tell them your plans. Most Embassies have a commercial section and usually have tons of contacts. They also arrange regular networking meetings where you can meet other ex-pats living and working in the country and swap business cards. These network meetings are by far the very best way to develop new contacts and then hopefully a few contracts, especially in hostile and high-risk environments where ex-pat communities are generally very close-knit. In most countries there is also a joint Chamber of Commerce with your home country; for example the Russo-British Chamber of Commerce is huge and extremely influential. The key for the first few weeks is to join as many business groups and Chambers of Commerce as you can, and attend all their network meetings. Also, most foreigners in high-risk environments generally live in protected compounds or specific guarded areas, and these are great ways to network too; knock on every door and say hello and make sure you attend the community's BBQ and get-togethers (although unfortunately in Moscow the BBQ season was not very long!). In almost every country there are also a few good bars and clubs where foreigners tend to meet and socialise, so use these to your business advantage and not just as a place to drink! Once again - using Moscow as an example - there were a couple of good watering-holes mainly frequented by Brits which, for me, were excellent places to meet other Brits. Every person I met I gave them my business card, and over the course of about a year I got a couple of really good security contracts just by chatting to people over a pint at the bar after work.

Another really good way of starting up in a foreign country, is to contact all the local providers of security and protection services and arrange to meet them. For legal and logistical reasons, for most operations you will probably have to work with a local security service provider anyway, but many local security companies just do not have the ability or the contacts to market their services to a generally much more influential and wealthier foreign client base. Therefore many will embrace the fact that, with a foreigner on their team (you), many more doors could be opened, providing an edge over their competitors. Plus of course, if you tie in with a local security company, setting up operations becomes infinitely easier than operating totally independently. I did this with two or three major security service providers in Moscow and it benefited all of us, considerably; I had the hardware (vehicles, firearms) and operational support of an established Russian security company, and they had the opportunity to work with a foreign client-base which they would never have been able to do on their own. It's a win-win situation.

I suggest that if you do decide to go abroad, whether alone or with other security colleagues, it is a very good idea to have enough money saved to live there for at least six months without working, as it will take a while to integrate into the ex-pat community, to get your name out there and to give enough people your business card and brochure. This doesn't happen overnight. When I first went to live in Moscow I had just sold my house in the UK and had a little spare cash, but I still lived a Russian life in a Russian apartment complex as it was far, far cheaper than living in a trendy ex-pat apartment. Again, make sure you do some research before you leave; find out about renting apartments, costs and conditions, and find out about the cost of living, travel, metro, car-hire, food etc. It took me about three months to get my first small contract, but once I got one, others followed pretty quickly thereafter. Websites were not around back then, so my business was built purely on word or mouth, but I established myself and eventually worked for some major blue-chip companies. Would I have worked with these clients back in the UK, even at a time when there were much, much fewer bodyguards on the circuit? Probably not.

Setting up in a high-risk part of the world is undeniably difficult, but not impossible, and it is definitely one hell of an adventure...

EXECUTIVE DRIVE TIME
By Tony Scotti

Consider that if an executive drove to and from the office, that time would be unproductive. What does that time cost the shareholders, and if the company supplies a Security Driver what is their Return on Investment (ROI)?

The answer to that question starts with - how much time is the Executive in a vehicle? A study done by Texas A&M titled the Annual Urban Mobility Report, answered that question for us.

Depending on the city, the Executive will be commuting from one to two hours a day. That does not count trips to the airport, meetings, and, at times, to evening activities. Also from the report an interesting statistic, a vehicle will be motionless in traffic 50 to 65 hours a year, which is only counting the commute time to and from work.

Working the numbers from the Texas A&M report, if the executive is in the vehicle for as little as an hour a day, considering a five day week, a 50 week year, they are in the vehicle 31.25 days a year. If the executive drove, he/she would be unproductive approximately a month a year, and that would be expensive.

What is one month of the executive's time worth in dollars? According to research conducted by the Associated Press which relied on data from Equilar, an executive pay research firm, the median compensation for a CEO in 2012 - the latest year for which a credible analysis is available - was $9.587 million. If one assumes the average number of hours worked on a weekly basis by an executive at this level is 60, then that executive's time is worth $3,072.75 per hour."

Using the Executive hourly salary provided by Equilar ($3072.75), if the Executive drove to and from work, and had one hour of non- productive Executive Drive time a day, it would cost the company $768,187.50 in a year. If the Executive drove to and from work, and had a total of 1.5 Hours of non-productive

Executive Drive time, it would represent a cost to the company of $1,152, 281.50 in a year. If the Executive drove to and from work, and had a total of two hours of non-productive Executive Drive time, it would represent a cost to the company of $1,536,375.00 in a year. Also, according to the study, and to make the driver's life more interesting, on an average, they will spend 24% of that time stuck in traffic. The Security/Executive Driver supplies the company with a significant return on investment. The end result is that a Security Driver is a good investment.

Why a Security Driver and not a Chauffeur?

The Risks
The executive sitting in the back seat of a vehicle is not like sitting at his desk either at the home or the office. Although the time may be minimal compared to other executive activities, Executive Drive Time also comes with risk, and as with all risks good business practice suggests these risks be understood and addressed.

When travelling by vehicle the executive is isolated, their location is constantly changing, and if there is a safety or security emergency, the only person that can assist the Executive, is the driver.

Although there are crisis management plans in place that offer Executive Drive Time Driving safety and security in the home and place of business, this safety/security envelope is breached during Executive Drive Time. Those risks are: The IRS, Medical, Vehicle Problems, Safety, Privacy, Security.

MORE ON LOOKING FOR WORK
By Robin Barratt

Let's face it, as I mentioned earlier, with over fifteen thousand licensed close protection officers in the UK alone, plus many thousands more with security degrees or other security qualifications, looking for work within this relatively small sector of the security industry will, for most people, be fairly difficult and for some, virtually impossible. Sorry to be so blunt, but these are the facts. Also, don't forget, if you are applying for international positions you are probably also competing with tens thousands of other well-trained and experienced close protection personnel worldwide.

But there is work out there and last month alone I found almost fifty positions advertised on the net (how many did you find?). The security industry worldwide is one of the few industries that has grown during this so-called 'credit crunch', and the threat level in almost every country worldwide has never been higher. Security is the number one concern for virtually everyone. Corporate businesses consistently spend an awful lot of money, and a great deal of time keeping both their business and its personnel safe.

And so, to be frank, the only person stopping you from finding work is actually... yourself! Maybe you don't have the right qualifications or experiences? Maybe you are not looking in the right places? Maybe you don't know where to look? Maybe you haven't joined the right forums or job search services or haven't submitted your CV to the right employment agencies or contractors? Or maybe you simply do not have the right attitude! The list - and excuses - for not finding work are endless. As I have said, having an SIA Close Protection license is not a guarantee of a job - it never was and it never will be - you have to do so much more and yet many people, not just in the UK but worldwide, will spend an awful lot of money on a close protection training course, get their badge or license and then virtually nothing thereafter on either further training or marketing themselves. Unbelievable but absolutely true. If you are saving for a course, save extra to market yourself once you get your badge!

Earlier we looked at being more specific as to what kind of protection you want to do, but you must also look at your Unique Selling Points (USP), which will help you considerably when it comes to looking for work. Ask yourself; what are your unique selling points, or in layman's language; what makes you different to the tens of thousands of other CPOs worldwide? If you say there is nothing different about me, it's about time you found something because, being one of fifteen thousand CPOs, won't get you very far in your job search. You need to stand out and to offer something that others don't have. Let me give you a few examples; a few years ago (before the SIA) I trained a coloured girl called Nicki. When she enrolled on my course, she had neither a military background, nor any security experience; in fact she started her career as a shop assistant! However, her goals were to set up a company providing black female bodyguards to black singers and celebrities. She did her initial basic CP training with me, and then further training with companies specialising in celebrity protection. She then took that knowledge and her training to further her career ambition and eventually started a female only security company in the US. Last year her company, based in LA, turned over about six million USD. She was black, she was female and she capitalized on her uniqueness, plus she had a set of defined goals and a vision of where she was going and exactly what she wanted to do. All this from a woman who was originally a shop assistant! She didn't use her background, or her colour as an excuse. Also, I once trained an Arab woman dressed in an Abaya (the long black robe-like dress, worn by some women in parts of the Islamic world) who has now gone onto work protecting many wealthy women from the Middle East. At the time, my uniqueness was operational support in Russia; I probably knew Moscow as well as I knew my home city which is what I capitalised on and marketed, and which immediately put me at a distinct advantage for anyone wanting security in

Moscow. So what is your unique selling point (USP)? Maybe you speak another language fluently? Maybe you have advance driving qualifications? Maybe you are a paramedic? Maybe you have previously worked in the precious metal or diamond mining industry? Perhaps you are a qualified scuba diver? Or maybe a mechanic? Or perhaps you know another country or major city really well? Maybe you stand head and shoulders above everyone else and built like a brick s**t-house and therefore ideal for high-profile celebrity work? I recently put two vacancies on a jobs list; one for a Portuguese speaking CPO and another for a CPO with an engineering background. Three months later the Portuguese vacancy still had not been filled - if your uniqueness was speaking Portuguese you would have been working out in the field! Find your uniqueness and market it, and if you don't have one, then get one! Make a list of five things that make you unique and which you can realistically use to find work within the CP sector, and then decide how you can use these USPs to achieve your goal in finding work. For example, maybe you speak Urdu, the fourth most commonly spoken language in the world, after Mandarin, English, and Spanish? There are between 60 and 70 million speakers of Urdu: around 52 million in India, 12 million in Pakistan and several hundred thousand apiece in the United Kingdom, Saudi Arabia, United States, and Bangladesh. This gives you a huge advantage - Pakistan for Westerners is one of the most dangerous countries in the world and rates Security Level 5. Saudi Arabia is not far behind, and as I mentioned earlier, United States employs the most bodyguards, so if you speak Urdu and live in the USA, you already have a massive advantage! An Urdu speaking CPO should never be out of work! As a CPO, if you have any form of paramedic or advanced first aid training you should never ever be out of work either; most contractors worldwide take paramedic trained CPOs in an instant. The same goes with CPOs with advanced defensive driving skills. Do you Scuba dive? There are loads of companies worldwide providing marine security desperate for scuba trained CPOs. Are you a former mechanic? Again you can find work easily in the Middle East where vehicles are constantly breaking down because of the extreme weather and sand. Are you a horse rider? I recently had a brilliant position sent to me as Head of Security at a stud in the Middle East, but he had to be a proficient rider (the position was not open to females). Are you a qualified close quarter combat instructor? Then training other CPOs in unarmed combat out in the field in high-risk areas can pay big money and I have found a number of vacancies for people with these skills. You must find something unique about yourself and market it as part of your portfolio, and if you have nothing unique other than just a basic SIA licence, than my advise would be; A) give up close protection or B) develop a speciality that interests you and quickly... because you ain't going to find much work otherwise!

As shown, I firmly believe it is better to specialise in one aspect of protection than to try and be a 'jack of all trades'. For example, if you develop a reputation as a specialist at Witness Protection then you become much more employable; people will actively seek you out because of your speciality. Because I was a specialist in Moscow, time and again I was asked to set up security operations in Moscow. When I lived in Bosnia in 1992 / 1993 - during the height of the conflict - time and time again, from journalists to aid workers, I was asked to look after people going into that arena. A good friend took various marine security courses as well as a couple of advanced anti-piracy courses, and now travels the world specialising in marine security - the last time I heard from him he was off the coast of Yemen (not floating)! Another friend, a former policeman, trained as a butler and then took a CP course and now, amazingly, works as a butler / security to a rich Arab family in Dubai earning a heaps of money doing a job he loves. Specialising works! Sometimes your hobby can lead to developing your USP. Make a list of three main areas of close protection and security you would be most keen to develop, for example: witness protection, protecting children, women, celebrity protection, event security, marine security, anti-piracy, canine, equestrian, paramedic, driving etc. Decide where you want to work, and in what sector and then add to this some of your own USPs, and there should be no reason at all to be out of work. Start to plan how you are going to do this... now. Or of course don't (because it is far too difficult?), and go back to stacking shelves or driving a bus. It is up to you!

Someone recently told me that they apply for every single job they hear about, regardless of whether they have the correct qualifications or experience or not. My jaw dropped. Why? I asked, and his reply was that if he walked down the street asking for £1, someone would eventually give him it. This maybe true begging on the streets, but sending his CV out to HR departments who neither have the time nor the inclination to read it, is wasting his time and reputation, but more importantly the time of the HR department! A good friend of mine who is currently working as Head of HR with one of the biggest security contractors in the UK, told me that he can receive up to a hundred unsolicited CVs each and every week. That's 5200 CVs a year! Unsolicited means that people are not applying for any specific position, they are just sending their CV on spec'. How does my friend who is extremely busy filling current vacancies and running his department have the time to read 5200 CVs that he has not even asked for? As I have said before, do not send your CV off blindly to as many people as you can! I got an email yesterday that simply said; "look at my CV attached and get back to me." Nothing else. Really professional huh? And then these people wonder why no one ever replies to them! As I have mentioned earlier, only send your CV to jobs for which you are suitably qualified; if you are not qualified then don't apply, simple. If a contractor gets a brief from its client about the position and the skills required, they won't change this criteria just because you happened to have sent in you CV without the appropriate qualifications / experience! Also, I met a CPO a few weeks ago and asked for his business card. He didn't have one but he scribbled his email address on a scrap of paper and gave it to me (and a stupid email address to boot!). Is this professional? Am I likely to keep this scrap of paper? You must get professional business cards printed with a professional sounding email address and a 24/7 contact number, preferably with a postal address too. You must have some way of letting people know who you are, what you do and how you can be contacted. You must view your business card as a mini brochure or flyer - it should sell who you are. Also, make sure the telephone number is available 24/7 - because people just do not call back after trying you once or twice, they will go elsewhere. If you have a voice-mail, make sure this is checked a couple of times a day too and call people back straight-away. A personal website is a really good idea too; they are very easy and quick to set up and nowadays you can easily edit and add to it yourself; long gone are the days when you needed a webmaster for even the simplest changes! Most domains costs less than £10 (16 USD) a year to buy, and most websites with online editing facilities costs around £10 a month. If you want some contacts for these let me know! The more professional you can look to a potential employer, the easier it will be to find that job.

EFFECTIVE NETWORKING
By Robin Barratt

Because there are so many CPOs now with close protection licenses - not just in the UK but worldwide - it stands to reason therefore, that a very large proportion of those people are actively looking for work. As I have already mentioned, every single day without fail, I receive emails and CVs from people either looking for work, or looking for tips and hints on finding work, or indeed asking me to find them work! Yes it's true, I actually get emails and Facebook messages from people I have never met, have never worked with, and who I don't know, ask if I could find them a job. Recently I had a message from someone on Facebook which simply read; *"Hello mate, can you tell me how I can find a job in CP."* That was it, nothing else! I didn't know him either. It happens time and time again; there are so many people that have absolutely no idea how to make that first step in searching for work, aside from sending off a quick message to someone they don't know, thinking that perhaps a quick reply would give them all the answers they need to kick-start their career.

When I started in close protection way back in the '90s, the job was certainly elitist and almost always based on referrals and recommendations. Networking was the key, and rarely did anyone go straight from a CP training course into regular employment if they were unknown. That was just the way it was. And actually, to a great extent, it is still the same today; the only difference now is that there are thousands more CPOs looking for work and so the necessity to network - not just after you have trained and have your license but from the very minute you make your choice of a career in CP - is infinitely more important. It was important back then and it is even more important today! But how do you get your name out there, how do you effectively network?

If you complain and moan that there is no work out there, for sure there will be no work out there! Guaranteed! And if you are not willing to network, not just on free forums but also by investing a little money on marketing your services, joining associations, subscribing to magazines, joining CP databases, and going to conferences and network events, it is unlikely you will ever find work. As I have mentioned earlier, you just cannot spend money on a CP course and nothing thereafter- if you did this you will certainly fail. But if you are consistently positive and pro-active, work will eventually come your way too. It is a bit like opening a shop; if you spend all your money on your stock, but nothing on telling people about it, it is doubtful you will sell much. But if you spend less on stock but a lot more on telling people about it, you can always order more stock when it runs out.

Knowing how to network and being a superb networker is the absolute key to successful job-hunting. Networking can be extremely useful for a whole number of things including: a) Learning about the politics and dynamics of a contractor, employer, principal or organization, b) Facilitating 'win-win' relationships (e.g. showing an employer that you are the best and highest qualified person for the position thereby everybody wins- you get the job, they get the best candidate and their client in happy), c) Establishing useful contacts, d) Building your referral networks, e) Giving and receiving advice, f) Developing CP community relations, g) Enabling your professional development opportunities, h) Seeking new opportunities in your career and beyond, i) Enabling the sharing of knowledge, j) Understanding how others have 'done it' and 'got the job' and k) Meeting people with different experiences and skills than your own.

Building an effective network does not occur by accident, nor does it happen overnight; to be a professional networker you need to work at networking every single day and keep a diary of what you have done, who you have spoken to and how they could help you - either now or in the future. You need to keep your eyes and ears open when events or opportunities to network present themselves and to make sure you are open-minded about where you network and who you speak to. Do not confine your possibilities to one and two main close protection forums and perhaps an annual security conference, or the occasional networking meeting, but networking should be done daily and the opportunities for this in this new media age are both endless and extensive. Through the internet and global social networks, you are connected to many more people than just those you meet in your local environment. Every one of your contacts has other contacts and they again have their own contacts, which may one day be beneficial for you. And that's just at the click of a button! The 'Human Web' connects you through a chain of 'a friend of a friend' to literally millions of others, and experiments have shown that you are on average approximately six steps or 'Six Degrees of Separation' away from any other person on Earth! And this is shown to be even less within specific communities such as close protection. The Head of the HR department for the biggest contractors in the world, employing tens of thousands of CPOs, knows someone, who knows someone who knows YOU! This is a fact, no matter where you live in the world, being within the CP community you will know someone, who knows someone, who knows someone who could be responsible for employing you.

Networking will change your life. My *Tough Talk* magazine quickly became the fastest downloaded magazine of its kind, all because of networking. However, it is very easy to find reasons not to network isn't it? It is easier not to attend that security conference or seminar - perhaps it costs too much or it's too far away, or maybe it's not really specific to close protection after all. It is easier not call someone to follow up after taking someone's business card; they were not really connected to close protection anyway. There are always excuses for not doing something, and it is far easier not to do something that to do it. Also, how do you really feel about networking? Does it make your nervous and awkward or are you comfortable making new connections? Not everyone enjoys networking or mixing with other people and, quite frankly, some people avoid it altogether. But once again, if you don't do these things, don't then complain that you can't find work, especially when most work is found via networking. Remember; networking can not only help you to find significant others that allow you to move forward in the CP world, but good networking can facilitate critical incidents that can change the course of your life! But if you would prefer not to network then it is likely you will never move forward regarding employment.

What are the key elements to effective networking?

The most important thing to remember is that first impressions count. Sounds obvious, but there are many people that forget this fundamental thing; research shows that people make up their minds about you in the first 30 seconds! It is important to ensure that you have a powerful way of introducing yourself to new people, because what you say and how you say it, will shape another person's impression of you in a few seconds as much as what you wear and how you behave. You may have been brought up to be modest, to keep yourself to yourself and be relatively retiring when it comes to promoting yourself, or telling others about your achievements but the truth is that if you want to increase your profile and reputation and successfully expand the network of people who have you on their radar, you have to actively work at it yourself both face to face, as well as through social networking sites, such as Facebook, Twitter, LinkedIn etc. People won't suddenly notice you - as if by magic! A winning network is based on actions, not words. It's a great feeling when someone says they will, for example, forward your CV to their colleague - and they actually do! It feels good for both parties. And these are the feelings you should be aiming for when networking; it's not just results but rewards, ratification and recognition.

It is also very important to have a clear focus about what you want to achieve, and a compelling rationale to ensure you achieve it. Before you leave for a security event, for example, think about what you want to get out of it. What type of people do you want to link up with and what information do you want to receive form them? It may be worth writing your goals down to keep you focused. Ensure you are organized and able to retrieve your business cards easily (don't fumble in your pocket or bag, for example). Be comfortable in what you wear and be aware that how you conduct yourself represents your personal brand. Also, make sure you use your time wisely. Don't stay talking to one person for too long, especially if this is one of your colleagues or friends. Develop your network strategically and meet a few new people every time you have the chance. This positive image will ensure that people take you seriously and know your challenges and ventures.

It is imperative to develop a powerful way of introducing yourself and again, make that first impression count! Don't talk about the weather and other 'nice' topics, instead, take interest in learning about the other person and find out about them. You learn so much more about what is happening out there by listening, as opposed to speaking. There is a saying; *"The wise speak because they have something to say, a fool because he has to say something."* Don't be the fool. When speaking about yourself, don't be afraid to talk about what your goals and objectives are. Doing your homework is another way of impressing people and always be honest; if you don't know something either admit it or ask, and don't try to fool or bluff by talking about things you don't know anything about, as you will get found out! It is much more impressive and appropriate to ask than waffling your way through a conversation and actually looking more like an idiot!

There is another well-known saying; *"It ain't what you know, it's who you know."* This rings true in the CP environment too! Successful networking needs to be cultivated. Make sure you remember who you met, what they said, who they are and what they do, and try to follow up by dropping them a 'good to meet you today' email or better still, telephone them a few days later. Then you have started to develop a networking relationship which could eventually develop into something significant. Also, develop an 'abundance mentality' as it's important to graze when mingling because you never know who else attending the meeting will be that ideal contact you will need down the line. However, if you are desperate to do everything at once it will show negatively.

Once you have started building the professional network that will help you in your future career, you will need to maintain it. Don't fall into the trap of circulating in 'clique' networks that include lots of people you already know; these are not as effective when you are developing your career. Instead, be adventurous and visit new people in new places - this is called disconnected networking.

Other important factors in networking:

- Take any and every opportunity to speak in public. If you specialise in a specific sector of security and protection, offer to speak free of charge at any and all networking events, conferences and seminars. The more people see you, the better it is!
- Write articles whenever you can and get them published.
- Join societies, associations, organisations and focus groups to maximize your potential contacts and even consider leading such societies to develop your skill set.
- Keep your details up-to-date, alter your CV every time you take on a new position or add to your training portfolio. Make sure you broadcast changes in your status to others as well.

Being smart and situationally aware enables achievement, as it puts you in the right frame of mind for action. This is the most optimistic and positive result you can achieve via networking. You must get to know the rules, customs and unwritten norms within different situations and within organizations. It's about understanding and being able to negotiate how things work in terms of networking, as well as finding your own genuine way of networking. For example, if it is a norm to get things done through developing relationships and it is not enough to purely put your head down and do a good job, it is critical to network. However, there may be times when networking doesn't come naturally; you don't feel authentic, you're forcing a smile or you're insecure about how to act and react. If this is the case you have to work at things to make you feel good by using your own skills, strengths and talents appropriately; you value self-development and progress; you are honest and inventive; you are creative and imaginative. You'll work it out!

The most successful networkers use their personal 'brand' when networking. Everyone is unique and has a 'brand' and your brand is your strengths, knowledge, skills, education, training and experience. These things bring credibility and gravitas when networking and it is what creates great first impressions. Good networkers usually stand out by differentiating themselves from the masses and you will find that others are always attracted to them; they are in demand. Be bold, be open, be approachable, be knowledgeable and have something to say as well as concentrate on listening to others.

Key points when networking:

Be Punctual. You don't want to have to give excuses for why you are late, no matter how valid. Plus, being late causes stress and you don't want that to ruin your positive mood. Plan to arrive at a networking event at least a few minutes before it starts to gather your thoughts and freshen up.

Be at Ease. If you get nervous before events - and many people do - consider relaxation or visualization, or you may prefer to play your favourite music track in the car on the way to get you in good spirits. If you are calm and positive and natural, others around you will feel the same. This gives you a solid foundation for making your first impression a good one. There's also an element of a 'just get on with it' approach that can also alleviate nerves.

Present Yourself Appropriately. This is common sense but it is said that a picture is worth a thousand words, and so the 'picture' you first present says much about you to the person you are meeting. You may not be a model but you can still create a strong and positive first impression by looking after your clothes and having a clean and tidy appearance is appropriate for most business and social occasions, combined with a good haircut or shave, clean shoes and tidy yet comfortable clothes. You'll be surprised how many people in the security industry don't follow these simple rules!

Demonstrate Your Individuality. As we have said earlier, it is vitally important to separate yourself from the thousands of other licensed CPOs! Tell people about your USPs; what makes you stand out in a crowd.

Be Confident. Be aware of your body language; you want to come across as confident and self-assured. Stand tall, smile, make eye contact, and use a firm handshake. One note of warning here, in some cultures and religions it is not appropriate to shake hands with someone of the opposite sex (eg some religious sects in the Middle East). On such occasions, waiting until the other person puts their hand out can be more advisable. Be aware of your nervous habits; control your nervous jitters or giddy laugh or mannerisms - being in control will develop your confidence and put others at ease.

Be Positive. Your attitude shows through in everything you do. Project a positive attitude, even in the face of criticism or in the case of nervousness. Strive to learn from your meetings and to contribute appropriately, maintaining an upbeat manner and a smile.

Be Polite and Conscientious. A polite, attentive, inquisitive and courteous manner will help make a good first impression. So remember to be on your best behaviour! Also, don't forget to turn off your mobile phone or at least put it on silent. It's very distracting when another person's phone rings, but it's embarrassing when it's your own! In a networking situation you need to give the person you are talking to your undivided attention.

Be Aware and Alert. To impress, you need to be aware and alert when mingling socially and professionally. You sell yourself as much by how you listen and react as by what you say and do. So watch, listen - not just to words but body language and facial expression - and try to empathize with the person in front of you. Sometimes you can make a terrific impression just by listening, keeping eye contact, nodding and saying just a few very incisive words.

Content v Body Language. So you're on time, at ease, dressed appropriately, confident, positive and conscientious. You know how to get to the point, but you still can't hit the bull's eye when networking! Well, next, you need to look more closely at your presentation and interpersonal skills because it's not always what you say but more likely how you say it that you're missing. Prof. Albert Mehrabian (1971) developed, from his research, a 7%-38%-55% rule for face-to-face conversations. Basically, what you say only matters 7% whilst 38% concerns your tone and 55% relates to your body language. Understanding non-verbal communication is, therefore, so important. And some people believe that it's now actually only 5% of what you say or content that matters and the rest is delivery. So the tone and pitch of your voice, your eye contact, body language, facial expressions need to be examined. The easiest way? Video yourself speaking and really see how you look and sound, and ask others for feedback as well.

Remember, before we even speak, we are already being judged on our appearance, body language, clothing and grooming and research shows that you have only a few seconds to make a good first impression, so it's well worth rehearsing the whole thing from entering the door to saying goodbye. If it's been practised, you are more able to give it your best shot. What you need to do is actually common sense but the thing is, through proper preparation, you can actually tailor your personal style for different occasions and make every first impression amazing!

Next, you need to consider some powerful introductions that really explain what you do. Remember, first impressions can influence the future actions or inaction of others, so make sure you work hard at deciding how you are going to impress them.

Once you have introduced yourself, what next? Pleasant conversation is nice, there's nothing wrong with talking about the weather or your next vacation, but is this how you wanted to spend you precious networking time at this particular event? Probably not! You need to be skilled at channelling the conversation towards your goals, shifting the focus to mutually beneficial areas and shepherding the subject matter. Here are some phrases that might make this happen, say…

- 'I just heard you mention you were recruiting for…'
- 'Have you thought of…'
- 'Can you tell me more about your current contract…'
- 'I was wondering when you are next recruiting…'
- 'I'd like to hear about the tender process…'
- 'I'm also working on a presentation about…'

Ask leading questions that prompt information based answers. Of course you want results and you have to be brave, sometimes even bold to ensure this happens, but make sure that you ask for things, don't demand. For example by saying ;'Tell me who to call'… you are demanding! Instead perhaps say; 'Do you know where I can get the telephone number for that organization?' Much better! You may be talking to someone who is always being asked for information, referrals and connections so go cautiously. Also, remember that people can be picky about who they help for selfish or other reasons. So sometimes, people may not want to network with you. Therefore, consider phrases like; 'I bet you get asked this a lot, can you forward me his e-mail address…' Or 'I hope you don't mind me asking…' Or 'I'm sure people contact you a lot in your position, but…' Maybe you'd like to meet them again to discuss things further. Think about saying: ' Do you have time to meet this week to discuss this further? Perhaps I could come to your office?' Or ' Do you think we could meet this week for a coffee?' Or 'Have you got time for a chat after the presentation?' Then, don't forget so say thanks without sounding patronizing. Try saying; 'Thanks for the chat. It was really useful.' Or 'You've been really helpful.' Or 'I really appreciate all your input.' It may be that you are asking for information they don't have at hand. In that case you may want to say; 'Would you mind if I call you this week to get that lead?' Or 'Could you text me the number later? Here's my card.' Or 'If you think of any suggestions, could you e-mail me?' On occasions, you may not be sure if what you are asking is inappropriate. For example, there's a fine line between asking for information and pestering a very busy person. It's also important to consider what you are asking for. In this case, honesty really is the best policy. Think about saying: 'Is it appropriate for me to ask for his mobile number?' Or ' I don't want to do anything unethical but if you could arrange for me to meet him/her, that would be great.' Or 'Is it appropriate for you to forward me the report?' It's about experimenting; having a go is the key thing.

We all see ourselves differently and we quite often misjudge how others see us. When you are new to networking, it's hard to be yourself, to be clear about what you want from your network and to give in return all at once. However, just like driving a car, where you initially find it overwhelming to handle the gears, mirror and steering wheel all at the same time, it comes together in time!

Determine which of your unique selling points will gain you more status and make sure you include that in your conversations. For example: 'I speak fluent Arabic', or 'I studied at so-and-so CP school', or 'I worked on a large project in Iraq with (name drop, people, company...)' etc. The skill here is developing the virtue of subtlety - weaving these points into a conversation. One tip is to use cues and take notice of people's body language. Stop if they are not interested. So, make sure that your unique selling points are not only interesting to the other person but that you sell them succinctly. No one likes waffle; it's boring and time wasting. A good 'sell' will entice the other person to ask you more. You may want to list a few of your talents in a row. Three points are usually enough though! Next you need to finish with fireworks. Leave your best point until last. People remember things that are outrageous, funny, sensual (related to smell, taste, touch, sound, and sight), and those connected to emotional experiences. In this respect, as people clamour for attention, you will be the one that's remembered. Here are some examples; I won employer of the year for three consecutive years, or I managed the largest CP team in the country, or I made Team Leader at the age of just 23 etc. It's all about gaining credibility, but be careful not to brag and don't lie!

Points To Remember:

- Maintain appropriate eye contact.
- Make your introduction sound effortless and natural.
- Be passionate and enthusiastic.
- Smile to show friendliness and enthusiasm.
- Provide a strong, firm voice to express confidence.
- Make it memorable and sincere.
- Sell your personality.
- Practice, write and rewrite your introduction.
- Including a compelling 'hook' to engage the listener and prompt them to ask questions.
- Be prepared to finish before the end of your mini-speech, if you see the listener's eyes closing of scanning the room too much.
- Practice your speech.
- Know your introduction inside out.
- End with an action request, such as asking for a business card or committing to sending an e-mail.

Remember the old saying; *"it's not what you do, it's the way that you do it"* that's truly what gets results! But results don't always happen overnight so persevere. Most importantly… *"Never, never, never give up."* Sir Winston Churchill, British Prime Minister and Nobel Prize Winner.

ANOTHER FEMALE'S JOURNEY INTO THE INDUSTRY
by Debbie Mills

In the Army, Deborah Mills served two operational tours of Northern Ireland and fought for Queen and Country in the second Gulf War. As a close protection officer, she worked in Iraq and was in charge of the Control Room when the British Council offices were attacked in Afghanistan. She also competed as a semi-professional boxer.

This is her story...

When I think back to my earliest childhood memory, I always recall one of my aunts saying to my mum Beryl; "Ber, can I take our Gorge out?" and my mother replying, "No!" Gorge was my nickname as a baby. When I asked my mother if this recollection was a memory, or just something I imagined, she replied; "Deb, that conversation did take place, but you were only about eleven months old!" I've heard that some people can recall memories from their childhood from around three and a half years-old, so I've defiantly defied the odds there. Or maybe my observation skills were present from my baby years and that's why I've chosen the career path I have. I wish my memory was that good now though; I struggle to remember what I did last week sometimes. But this could be due to a few occurrences in my life so far; the heavy alcohol consumption in my early years as a soldier for HM Armed Forces in Germany, the stressful and dangerous situations I've been involved in during Service in the Second Gulf War and as a private bodyguard to the Foreign and Commonwealth Office in Iraq and Afghanistan, or maybe as a semi-professional boxer... I just took one too many punches to the head!

I was born on 16th October 1979, and grew up in a small suburb called Rock Ferry, on the Wirral, not far from Liverpool. My childhood wasn't the best, but it most certainly wasn't the worst either. There was a lot of arguing between my parents, metaphorical 'bloodshed' and tears between my family members. But isn't this what every family goes through, especially when you grow up in a deprived area where unemployment levels are high and expectations low? The arguments would always start on a Friday or Saturday night, after my mum and dad had been out drinking. I would dread the sound of the front door as they returned home, as it always woke me from my sleep and I knew what was coming next. I would lay in my bed next to my younger sister (I have two sisters; one younger and one older, and an older brother), hoping that my parents would stop shouting at each other before they woke her up. But they never did, and it always took me to go downstairs and beg them to stop. At a young age I never knew what they argued so much about; sometimes it was so bad that my mum would get me and my sister up out of bed and we would flee to my aunt's house. I recall one night in particular, when the arguing got really bad and my older brother intervened and pinned my father down on the settee, while me, my mum and younger sister fled and ended up hiding in a graveyard close to where we lived, until a taxi came and picked us up. I remember thinking I should be scared right now, but instead I felt excited. I think I must have been born with a sense of adventure and danger and now, I only feel fully satisfied in a job or sport where both of these things come into play. I don't blame it on my childhood though, I think it's just how I'm made.

  The arguing and fighting got worse into my teenage years and I got more brazen in dealing with it. I would swear, yell and scream at my parents to stop, even on one occasion fronting up to my father telling him I'd had enough and why didn't they just split up if they hated each other so much, instead of putting me and my younger sister through all those sleepless nights.

  I've never told my parents this, but the reason I joined the Army was to get away from the arguing; a selfish act really, as that left my younger sister to deal with all the arguing and fighting alone. But I just had to get out.

  I honestly couldn't tell you how a 'normal' family is supposed to be, but all I know is that, aside from the arguing, fighting and tears, my parents loved me unconditionally and they are now like best-friends; the arguing and fighting is a thing of the past. They have supported me through every part of my life, and I know how proud they are of me and I want them to know that, regardless of my childhood, they have made me the strong, determined and ambitious woman I am today. The saying; 'What doesn't kill you, makes you stronger' couldn't be more true; I'm the living proof.

Actually though, I never had any intention whatsoever in joining the Armed Forces. It all started with me and my friend H going into an Army Careers office in Birkenhead for a laugh. We ended up coming out with an information pack and a parent's consent form to complete an application to join, as I was still only sixteen. I remember taking it home and telling my parents I was going to join the Army, they signed the papers, but I don't think for one minute they thought I would ever go through with it. But just a couple of weeks later I found myself once again sitting in the career's office with H, as we attempted our BARB (British Army Recruit Battery) tests to see what Corps and trades we could apply for. I didn't find the test particularly hard but to my disappointment I only scored enough points to apply to be a driver in the Royal Logistic Corps, but I wasn't too bothered - I was more excited about the prospects of travelling the world and getting my driving licence, as well as learning an abundance of other key life skills I would never get living in Rock Ferry.

A few weeks later I was standing nervously at Lichfield train station waiting for a scary Corporal to shout my name, so I could board a minibus and go to attempt my fitness and medical tests to join the British Army. I remember one lad turned up in a tracksuit, and the Corporal screamed at him, from about a millimetre away from his face, telling him to phone his parents to come and collect him, as he was not correctly dressed or smart enough to join Her Majesty's Armed Forces. The lad was in tears, which appeared to infuriate the Corporal even more. I eventually got my name called out and froze as the Corporal assessed whether I was correctly dressed. I had on one of my dad's shirts and a pair of school trousers and blazer, but it worked and I made it on to the minibus.

I passed the medical, and all parts of the fitness test apart from the upper body strength test - four assisted heaves; where you start in the sitting position on the floor, then lift your upper-body so that your chest touches the beam, your legs raise in a vertical position but your feet remain on the floor. When I was called in for my final interview, the Officer in Command told me I had failed assessment and would have to come back in six months time. I was devastated. I felt so deflated and, as I returned home on the train that afternoon, thought to myself; 'you can do this Deb, get training on you upper body strength and go back in six months and pass with flying colours.'

And that's exactly what I did. On 24th April 1997, I was sworn in under Oath into the Royal Logistic Corps, HM Armed Forces and, a couple of weeks later, sent to Pirbright in Surrey to undergo eighteen weeks Basic Army Training.

The first six weeks we were 'beasted' from one corner of the camp to the other, and taught the very basics of teamwork, and when someone didn't make their bed or clean the toilet with a toothbrush correctly, we were all punished. I made some really good friends during this period, and we helped each other through the hardest of days. It was real comradery; the majority of us worked hard together as a team and the ones who didn't either left because they couldn't hack or they were chucked out because they just didn't make the grade. After those initial six weeks we were moved into the main accommodation block, and were given a proper uniform, instead of the lovely green coveralls we had worn since we arrived.

The following twelve weeks were some of the best times of my life; I grew more confident, I felt fit and strong and found that I was able to do things I never thought I would ever be able to do. One of my closest friends through basic training was JG; we were so alike, both jokers, and spent nearly every room-inspection giggling away or trashing each other's beds five minutes before the Corporal was due to carry out an inspection. Whenever one of us got into trouble, the other was always there, which usually resulted in the Corporal marching us off around the drill square.

I passed out of Army Training Regiment, Pirbright, and was then sent to Deepcut Barracks to complete my Phase 2 training, which included learning how to drive a car, HGV vehicle and HGV with trailer. I passed all of those and became fully qualified and ready for deployment to my first Army unit.

I remember my last day at Driver Training School. It was a Friday and I thought I would be allowed to go home, before returning to Deepcut to be posted - I had planned a weekend at home and was looking forward to seeing my family and friends. I went to the Administration building to hand in my pass certificates, but when I got there, they told me I would have to be on a bus back to Deepcut on that Saturday morning. I was gutted. I had arranged a lift from one of the girls, so I hid in her boot of her car, and spent the weekend at home after all. Monday morning was spent being quick-marched around the camp.

Fast forward a month and I had arrived at 617 Headquarter Squadron, 7 Transport Regiment, Bielefeld, Germany, and was about to embark on what was most defiantly the most drunken years of my life. I should have known what was to come when, that very first night, I was told to present myself in the Squadron bar to be initiated; I had to stand on a table and recite the phonetic alphabet, whilst drinking a yard of beer and three pints of traffic-light-coloured drinks. I made it through, but funnily enough don't remember much more of that night.

During my four years based in Bielefeld, I served two operational tours of Northern Ireland, was on exercise Saif Sareea in Oman, and went on a football tour of America with the British Army Women's Football Team.

One of the things I do recall clearly from my time in Germany is how I cheated death. Along with a few other girls, I was due to go to the UK represent the Regiment in basketball but, at the very last minute, was told I couldn't go as I was going on a training exercise with the squadron. I was gutted; I was looking forward to going to the UK for a week. A few days later we learned that there had been a road traffic accident; three of the girls had died and four were seriously injured. RIP girls, gone but never forgotten.

After four years in Germany, I felt it was time to come back to the UK and asked for a posting back in England, and I was attached to 33 Field Hospital in Gosport, Hampshire. I had been promoted to Lance Corporal in Germany, so my post was in a small five-strong Royal Logistic Corps Detachment, where my role was to co-ordinate and lead on radio communications. It was in this posting that every soldier's wish came true; I got the opportunity to deploy to Iraq and fight for Queen and Country in the second Gulf War.

We arrived in Kuwait in early March, about two weeks before the war was actually officially declared on 20th March 2003. It was quite surreal at first, as the missiles started getting fired at us and we would go through the drill of donning our respirators and NBC suits and getting into cover in the trenches. But, as the days passed, it became the norm and the temptation to stay in bed after the alarms sounded continuously throughout the night became stronger. I remember one particular attack very clearly; we had all been moved from the trenches to a chemical protection tent, as there was concern one of the missiles had been a chemical weapon. Once in the tent, we all sat and waited for the 'all clear' to be given, I noticed a young female officer next to me struggling for breath in her respirator. As we didn't know whether the missile had been a chemical one or not, I immediately thought; 'Shit, is this it, she's contaminated.' As she continued to struggle for breath, she was showing all the potential signs that we had been hit by a chemical weapon and I remember thinking; 'Don't panic, stay calm.' It seemed like forever, but it was only seconds, until the Regimental Sergeant Major came over, lifted off his own respirator, and tended to the young officer. We all gasped as we thought he would immediately start to feel the effects of what we thought was a chemical weapon attack and were relieved when, through gasping breaths, she said she was having an asthma attack and needed her inhaler.

I was deployed on Operation Iraqi Freedom for approximately three months. It was a real wartime experience, and one I will never forget; it taught me the fundamentals of coping in extreme hostile situations and how camaraderie and friendship can get you through the toughest of times. But one thing I never really considered at that time was the impact of me being at war had on my parents and family; every time a missile was fired or a bomb dropped I knew *I* was fine, but my parents and family had to endure the television news bulletins and await that dreaded phone call. Most of my working career has been in hostile environments, and my parents, family and partner have had to re-live those feelings of fear over and over again.

Fast forward two years and four months and I had finally come to the end of my Service and, with only two days left in Her Majesty's Armed Forces, had made the decision to leave the Army. The main reason was that I had met Jemma, the love of my life, who was a civilian and lived back in Liverpool, and I was sick of being away from her all the time. Also, I was plagued with a football injury that had resulted in my anterior cruciate ligament being reconstructed, and I knew that if I stayed in the Army, I would be medically downgraded for a long time whilst I recovered, which would then affect my promotion and career prospects. Plus, to be honest, I'd really just had enough of being told were to go and what to do, and I wanted to be just more than a number.

I was due to leave Sandhurst as a civilian on Thursday 7th July, 2005, making my way from Sandhurst station to Reading, and then onto London Paddington in order to get the Underground to Euston around 0900, but a dental appointment on my final medical had put me back a day; I was suffering from toothache which turned out to be an abscess on a root canal filling and I had the opportunity of getting the tooth removed on Friday morning and then I'd travel home, so I decided to stay the extra day and get the tooth sorted.

I don't think I need to highlight what happened in London on Thursday 7th July, 2005, particularly on the Paddington bound train that morning - it was the United Kingdom's first suicide style attack and the worst terrorist attack since the Lockerbie bombings in 1988. God rest every soul that died that day and to all the survivors who live each day; you are all heroes in my eyes and I hope each day gets a little easier for you.

Since my nan had passed away in 1997, I always felt like she was watching over me and I know it sounds a bit strange, but when I think back to things that have happened to me over the years and in hostile and difficult situations, it's clear to see I definitely have a Guardian Angel, and I'm sure it's my Nanny Betty. I count myself very lucky that I have somehow managed to avoid potentially life-threatening events and, especially after the London bombings, have always thought; did these events shape my future career choices? Did I like to play devil's advocate because of my longing for a job with excitement and an element of danger? Was it because I had avoided those two key events in my life, where my life could have ended - the London bombings and the vehicle crash – that I felt I was invincible?

After the Army, I spent the first two years as a civilian working for a predominantly ex-military company in Primary and Secondary Schools across Merseyside with disaffected and disadvantaged children aged nine to fifteen years-old. It was an enjoyable job, and I actually earned more money than I did as a Corporal in the army, but I got bored as I was pretty much doing the same thing every day. I enjoyed working with the more 'harder to reach kids' but even if he or she goes to school and is given the right attention and guidance to do well, they then go home to parents who don't really care about them, you're fighting a losing battle.

In May 2007, I attended a First Aid Instructor course and met a couple of lads working in close protection. They had worked in Iraq as private security contractors, and as we chatted about what they had done and the money they earned and I started immediately thinking 'I could do that.' When I got home I had a chat with Jem and asked her what she thought. Jem has always supported me through absolutely everything I have achieved in my life and, although I've taken her to hell and back, she's always been there to encourage and support me in whatever choices I've made. So in October 2007, I touched down in Erbil, Northern Iraq, as a Close Protection Operator for the British Consulate Office.

To be totally honest, the eighteen months I spent there were very quiet; it was more of a residential security role, we were based in a hotel and rarely went out. After about nine months I took the position of Medic / Medical Trainer, but the worst it ever got was sticking a needle in a hairy arse to calm sickness for someone with diarrhoea and vomiting, and so I jumped at the chance of 'getting some action,' when a vacancy appeared in Afghanistan at one of the biggest British Embassies in the world, and by January 2009 I was driving around Kabul taking diplomats and other governmental staff to locations for meetings and their day-to-day business. It was fast-paced, dangerous and exciting, and everything I longed for in a job. This first stint in Afghanistan only lasted a little under six months and I returned to the UK for a while, but it wasn't long before I was back on route to Afghanistan but this time, however, it was going to be a lot more than I bargained for, and I was really going to experience the toughest times of my life and career.

The flight from Manchester to Dubai was a really bumpy one, so I wasn't looking forward to boarding Safi Airways from Dubai to Kabul, as that journey was always like a roller-coaster, but I managed to meet up with a few of the lads I'd previously served with, so it was good to have company on the way in. This time had been particularly hard leaving Jem though, and I was feeling low, but I tried to focus on just getting the first nine week rotation out of the way, and using the money to get rid of our final few debts. When I first thought of doing close protection in the Middle East, I made a promise to myself not to do anymore than five years, as it was so easy to get stuck in that world, constantly spending the money earned on expensive holidays and not really planning for any future. I too had fallen victim to this mindset during those first three years and foolishly blew all the money I had earned. I lived each day as it came, not really knowing which one would be my last.

The next event that unfolded in Afghanistan, on 19th August 2011, really changed my whole outlook on working in the Middle East, and it finally hit home that the danger I was putting myself was worth no amount of money.

I was working alone, running the Embassy operations room. It was nearly at the end of a night shift when, at 06:15, I heard a very loud explosion - our British Council offices had been attacked. A suicide car bomb had destroyed the compound wall and a number of heavily armed men forced their way inside killing at least twelve people. I received the initial phone call from a colleague who was in the Council offices and under attack, and I literally had minutes to try and respond effectively and to get as much support to him as possible, whilst still managing the Ops Room and getting the necessary staff to assist with the management of the incident. Every phone was ringing and I had to make sure my actions were correct and swift. I tried to keep my colleague calm on the mobile line, whilst trying to make announcements and get the relevant Quick Reaction Forces into action. It seemed like hours, but in reality it only took minutes before the Operations Manager ran in, and then other people started to arrive to assist. The attack went on for eight hours and sadly we lost a few local Afghan security guards who had bravely defended the British Council offices but who had been caught up in the first explosion, and a New Zealand Special Forces soldier who was shot during the eight hour stand-off. It was the most difficult situation I have had to manage, and holding a phone speaking to someone hiding in a Safe Room, while terrorists tried to gain entry or blow themselves up, was the most daunting and emotional situation I have ever faced; the responsibility to get them out safely relied on the initial actions I carried out. Eventually we managed to extract my colleague and two clients from the Safe Room when, at the very moment they were extracted, the battery died on his mobile that we had been talking on for eight hours. I was so relieved to see him at the Embassy later.

As the event unfolded, RPGs (Rocket Propelled Grenades) were fired randomly from derelict buildings close to the Embassy, where insurgents had taken up positions and were targeting foreign nationals. It was then that I really started to think that one day I might not go home. So I made the decision to finally leave behind my close protection days in the Middle East and return home to my partner and family, and stop putting them through the agonising news flashes of attacks in Kabul and not knowing whether I was dead or alive.

I've been back in the UK since February 2012, and have worked as a Security Manager during the Olympic Games responsible for security teams at Downing Street, St James Palace and other royal venues, as well as short term contracts providing personal security to a number of high-net worth individuals and on governmental sites across the UK. I also took up semi-professional boxing and, although only short lived (mainly due to my age), I managed to have an area title fight which I lost on points to a very tough opponent, who is also a good friend. I'd started training for boxing competition while in the UK, after my first Afghanistan posting, and continued to train hard whilst out in Afghanistan. One of my most enjoyable experiences was meeting an Afghan boxing coach, when the then British Ambassador took me along to a pre-Olympic event where I ended up sparring a female Afghan boxer. We became good friends, along with the three other female boxers who represented Afghanistan in China when trying to qualify for the 2012 London Olympic Games. They were true, tough, strong women and I hope they achieve their dreams of boxing and living in peace. I still keep in touch with them and their coach, and am planning to bring them to the UK one day so that they can experience training in a safe environment without the threat of their lives being taken, just for doing something they enjoy.

I'm still with Jemma and am settled in a great management job, and run an amateur boxing club for Derry Mathews, a local professional boxer who will be a World Champion very soon! I am also planning to write a book based on some of my experiences living and working in hostile environments. But, whatever the future now holds for me, I hope women will be inspired that a kid from Rock Ferry, Wirral, can go onto achieve and experience some of the things I have, and that they too will be motivated to go out there and live their dreams, whatever they maybe.

Whatever life throws at me I follow one simple motto,

tattooed on my back; 'to do one's best.'

***

Extract from the book ***Britain's Toughest Women - Some of the toughest women bodyguards, bouncers, bodybuilders, boxers, martial artists and MMA fighters in the UK****. Available now as a paperback: ISBN: '978-1508941262 and Kindle: ASIN: B00WA7OT0S.*

CAN DOOR SUPERVISORS MAKE GOOD BODYGUARDS?
By Robin Barratt

It is estimated that around 65% of the current 15,226 close protection licenses are held by either former, or serving door supervisors, with 25% from former military (with no other security experience), and only 10% pure civilians with no military background or security experience. This means over 8000 CP licenses are held by door supervisors! Yet if you ask most of the principal international operational security companies and contractors if door supervisors can make good bodyguards, most would say definitely not! Most former military and special forces personnel would probably say exactly the same thing - albeit a little more bluntly. Regardless of your ability and aptitude, or your training and experience, if you're a former doorman and happen to make it into a CP team with an ex-military or special forces colleague, and you tell him that you were a door supervisor, you would quickly find yourself transferred to twelve-hour shifts minding a muddy corner of the garden in the middle of nowhere... in the pouring rain. Even though the majority of licenses are held by door supervisors, few operating in close protection are door supervisors and, even though the industry has changed immeasurably over the past few years, there is still an ingrained mindset that all door supervisors are twenty-stone, tattooed, mindless thugs unable to put a few sentences together, let alone able to work out the logistics of planning and implementing a professional international close protection operation.

I once sent an email to someone on my database notifying him of the release of my earlier magazine *On The Doors*. He replied almost immediately by saying he works in close protection and would never ever, ever... ever involve himself in anything to do with the doors or door supervision, and to take him off my database immediately! Knob. This attitude shows that there is still so much stigma against door supervisors entering the protection industry. Yet without the hundreds of door supervisors paying for close protection training, many training companies (actually most!) would have quickly gone out of business. In fact, it is because of the huge door supervision market that there are now many more companies than ever offering close protection and related training. I recently visited a CP course run by a well-known and respected company in the East of England where almost all their students were door supervisors aside from just two from the military and one civilian. Admittedly, even with licensing, there are still many mindless morons out there working the doors, as well as quite a few foreign mindless morons that cannot speak English working the doors too (but that's another story!), but aside from these idiots, the door supervisor industry has changed and there are now many more bright, intelligent 'ordinary' people working the doors and using door supervision as a stepping stone into the security industry, including close protection. If you walk through a typical town on a Saturday night you will find that most door supervisors are in fact neither twenty-stone nor mindless; most you can have a decent conversation with, most are generally approachable and most have other jobs and career aspirations that many of the 'old school' doormen didn't have - no offence to old-school doormen!

Regardless of whether you are a door supervisor or a former Officer of the SAS, what it takes to be a bodyguard is exactly the same; complete commitment to the job, absolute dedication to your principal and team, a high and sustained level of concentration and, of course, a strong desire to succeed, but ultimately a compulsive motivation to protect; you cannot be a bodyguard and be willing to put yourself in real harm's way for someone you hardly know, if you do not have a sincere and tangible instinct to protect. It doesn't just take former Paras, Marines or SAS soldiers to be able to conform to these basic principles, nor does it mean that just because you have had military training that you automatically conform to that criteria either. A well-educated, well-disciplined, conscientious doorman (or woman) can be as good a bodyguard as anyone, and there is a large number of cases where former door supervisors are successfully working in teams in both low and high-risk environments around the world. A good friend of mine who used to run a few doors in Edinburgh, has been working consistently in Iraq running his own CP team since the war began, and is now Chief Instructor and Team-Leader for a multi-national security contractor. Another former doorman and friend is now running a prestigious security division for the United Nations in Africa. A former door woman I know well is currently heading a team based in London looking after Middle Eastern clients. The list is endless. Door supervisors can, and do, make excellent bodyguards, but it is their ability that has rewarded them, not the fact that they were, or were not, door supervisors. And surprisingly, when chatting recently to a couple of well-known UK based companies about this subject, a few said that they actually prefer to employ non-military personnel for their low-risk, low-profile operations. According to them, this is because former military types can stand out and are sometimes far too regimented for a civilian security environment, especially those from a Special Forces background. And they said that many former Special Forces soldiers were mental; off their trolleys, difficult to manage and too arrogant for the civilian sector (no... really?). Due to the fact that the risks posed within some environments are very similar to those working on the doors - something which former SAS personnel know little or nothing about - door supervisors work especially well with celebrities and at special events including film premiers, music festivals, private parties and corporate events. But, at the opposite end of the scale, door supervisors know little or nothing about war-zone environments and this is where former soldiers excel; instinctive trained reaction is undoubtedly a life-saver in contact situations and our modern British society (at the moment anyway), gives little opportunity to develop instinctive reactions in life-threatening situations. For example, one of my jobs in Bosnia during the conflict was to pick up 'volunteers' from Zargreb airport and take them onto the front-line. Boastful, bragging, loud-mouthed doormen (and believe me, there were quite a few of them!) were generally the first to return home within just a couple of days once the first bullet whizzed past their ears, or mortar exploded nearby. Whereas the quiet humble soldier would last for many, many months out in the field. I have witnessed a real hard-looking tattooed twenty-stone doorman literally crap his pants at the first incoming mortar attack, yet a bespectacled *Times* crossword loving, ex-SAS soldier stay undercover in Serb territory doing all sorts of 'interesting' things for months and months. It is not your background that is important, but your attitude.

As one highly regarded and respected security consultant with many years of international experience once said: *"I now think the CP world is becoming a complex environment as the evolution brought about by the high-risk (war zone) protection roles has expanded the role beyond the traditional executive or celebrity protection. The 'rules of engagement' have moved away from the 'minimal force' adopted in a typical western [or law abiding] society into more of an offensive or aggressive precautionary attitude. Overt escorting of engineers in Iraq is worlds apart from a discreet protection provided to a senior banker in London. I see the Iraq type service being a reactive and emergency management process, whereas the London based role is all about planning out the risk, educating those around the principal and working with society to avoid placing the principal in dangerous situations. However, in Iraq, you are always in a dangerous environment and it is how you manage the situation once it becomes lethal (bomb, shooting or enraged crowds) that defines success. Too many people are 'experts' and the average client finds it very hard to separate a corporate EP specialist from those ex-soldiers who have spent time in a war zone. These are two different roles requiring two different sets of skills, some of which have shared origins but different delivery methods. I'm a snob and I think the industry has regressed since the SIA got involved; all we have done is created a plethora of training companies who all offer widely differing standards of service. This is why the debate about the meaningless license will prevail for some years to come".*

Close protection isn't just about high-risk assignments in

battle-grounds and war-zones and, as long as you are completely dedicated to the industry, confident and have an ability to learn and to follow orders, there is a place for both door supervisors and ex-soldiers throughout the close protection industry. And as long as you are realistic about where you want to work, and with whom, door supervisors can, and do make very good bodyguards.

HOW TO WRITE A GOOD CV
By Robin Barratt

There are many, many CPOs who amazingly still refuse to spend any time - or money - on a good quality CV. This is just unbelievable! Your CV is the first thing any employer will see. Your CV is your gateway to employment; without a CV you cannot get any work and without a good CV you will never get invited to an interview. Everyone, at every level of the industry, will need a well written, relevant CV in order to find work; it is as simple as that. However, after over 25 years in the industry, I am still amazed how many appalling CVs land on my desk each and every week.

The purpose of your CV is to open doors; your objective being to get to an interview, and then it is your skills at interview which will decide your career path; whether in close protection or stacking shelves at Tesco. A really good CV should eventually land you a really good job and so it is vitally important that you spend time and money getting your CV absolutely right - it is the window to employment and it is the only chance you will ever have to get your foot in the front door. Don't make mistakes with your CV!

Many people try - badly - to do a CV themselves or ask a friend or family member. There are also loads of people who go to a professional CV service advertised in their local newspaper. Undoubtedly these companies are very good at writing CVs for everyday, normal, employment, but applying for jobs in close protection is very different to a normal job, and understandably most professional CV services have little or no knowledge or understanding of what is required in the world of close protection. There is nothing wrong with using a CV service, but if you do, make sure you use a company with experience in the security sector and / or CP.

So, what makes a bad CV? I have seen CVs littered with spelling mistakes and really obvious grammatical errors, which is unbelievable in this computer-led day and age. In every language, every word-processing system on every computer, everywhere in the world has a spelling and grammar check facility with mistakes highlighted by your PC in either red (spelling) or green (grammar), so make sure these settings are on and that everything is spelt perfectly and the grammar is correct. If a possible employer sees that there is bad grammar in such a simple document as your CV, what will he think your grammar will be like with report writing, form-filling and the general administration a CPO has to deal with? Also, there are things that do not show up on spell-checks including; 'of' and 'off,' there' and 'their', 'its' and 'it's', 'our' and 'are' , 'know' and 'now.' Do you know the differences? If you don't, find out! You would not believe the number of CVs out there (not out their) with these simple mistakes! Also careful when mixing American and English spelling, e.g. traveling and travelling, specialize and specialise etc. Try to chose either one, or the other, but not both and if you are in any way unsure then ask someone with a good knowledge of the English language to proofread your CV before sending it out to potential employers. But never proofread it yourself, because you will read what is in your mind and not what is actually written on the paper. Pay a professional proofreader to proof it for you, they will only charge a small amount for a couple of pages but it will be well worth it.

When writing your CV, you should only detail what is relevant to security. For example, would an employer for a high-risk close protection assignment in Nigeria be interested in the fact that when you were seventeen years old you spent six months stacking shelves at Tesco? Or that you took a year off work in your early twenties because of depression? Or that you chaired the Durham Town Netball Club? I have actually seen these very examples, and many, many more besides, on CVs coming into my office. I have also had five, six, even seven page CVs that go into so much irrelevant detail e.g.: *My wife thought I should change my job because of the pressure of coming home late in the evenings and not being able to spend as much time as possible with my family....* Seriously, this was written in one CV I received.

A CV should be two to three pages at most, and should only detail the facts, excluding emotions / reasons / excuses etc., and it should only detail what is absolutely relevant to the security industry. Don't write that you stacked shelves, worked as a plumber or anything not specific or related to security and close protection. Employers are not interested; remember, applying for a position in close protection is very different to applying for most normal jobs.

Everyone writes in their personal profile: *'I am a hard-working individual, who is both a team-player and able to work on my own initiative ...!'* Let's face it; you are not going to write that you are a lazy bastard who hates other people and is scared shitless in any environment remotely threatening. If you are going to write a personal profile (by the way, you don't have to if your CV is excellent!), try to think of something unique and different, and put your profile at the end of the CV, not at the beginning. Let your possible employer read the essential facts about you first: your background, experience, training etc., and not a personal profile which is exactly the same as everyone else's! Look at things from the HR's perspective; most people working in busy HR departments don't have much time and they get hundreds of CVs each and every week, so the quicker you can present the most important details, the more likely it is that your CV then gets read without being binned, which then means you are a little bit more likely to get to the next stage of the application process. I throw away more CVs than I read, simply because I am not captivated immediately, and I don't have the time to wait in the hope that perhaps I might be captivated and I don't have the time to waste if I am not. So make sure your CV holds its readers' attention straight-away.

So what should you detail in order to hold the readers' attention? It is a fact that most people working within the high-risk close protection environment have a military or services (police etc.,) background. Many working in lower-risk environments e.g. events, concerts etc., are door supervisors and from the general private security sector. So, if you are applying for high-risk roles then of course your CV should first detail your military / services career, as this is what most employers immediately look for. Having some sort of a military background significantly increases the chances of finding work in CP so if you particularly want to work in the high-risk arenas but don't have any military experience, then get some... join the Territorial Army or Reservists!

On your CV you should then ideally detail your career in close protection in chronological order, with your present position first. After your career list your CP training and any related security industry training. Lastly list your personal profile (if you want to) as well as any other information relevant to the industry e.g. languages, scuba diving skills, horse riding etc. However, if you are a specialist, then I strongly advise putting your speciality at the very beginning of your CV, label it accordingly e.g. Specialist in Marine, Anti-Piracy and Ship Security, and then angle your profile accordingly.

It is vital that you only detail what you can prove. I had a CV a few years ago from someone saying he had worked in Moscow. I was living in Moscow at the time and called him to find out more, as I was looking for a few people with operational experience in Russia. It transpired that he didn't actually work in Moscow at all; he was on the way home and never left the transit lounge of the airport. Another time I had a call from someone saying they had worked the oil fields on the outskirts of Moscow, and who unsurprisingly was extremely embarrassed when I told him the nearest oil fields were thousands of kilometres away in the Caspian Sea. He also said that he spoke basic Russian but when I asked how he was - in Russian - he couldn't answer. Don't bullshit on your CV and don't detail anything that isn't true or cannot be verified; just detail the facts. Also don't state the obvious. I get hundreds of CVs from people with SIA licenses detailing exactly what their CP training comprised off! I know what SIA accredited training comprises of, and so does every major contractor, so why detail that you have learnt embuss / debuss / PES drills etc. Of course you have, otherwise you would not have your SIA license! However, you must detail your course syllabus if the course is not recognised, or you have trained in a different country or using different systems, equipment etc.

Lastly, I would suggest not to send a photo with your CV at first unless the job application specifically states it. The reason is that some people are just not photogenic and initial decisions might be made on the look of the applicant rather than their qualifications and experience. And make sure your contact details are updated - and that you are contactable - you would not believe the number of CVs I get with email addresses that are returned, or mobile numbers that are either never answered or not connected.

HOW MANY CVS HAVE I RECEIVED THIS WEEK!
By Tony Fithon

How many CVs do I get each and every week? It never stops! but hey, this is the game we are all in and yes, you must keep looking and pushing for the few jobs that are available. But what makes your CV different from the rest? And what makes it jump out and say "READ ME" and not put in 'file 13' with all the others that have not caught my eye,? Quite simple; honesty, less garbage / bull, but most of all... qualifications!

So let's say you have got your CV to the right person (a mission all of its own), and let's say you get called for that interview, then great, but what has actually got you to this stage?

In my opinion it's not only the neat and tidy CV, or the picture attached that shows you smart as a carrot, fit and with your piercings left in the bathroom, but the attached qualifications that tells future employers (and me) that we don't need to spend a penny on training you further, as you have more qualifications than both Batman and Superman put together.

As the Managing Director of a security company that has had several multimillion pound contracts, both in the UK and overseas, and having personally served over twenty years in the military, believe me I know how hard it is to get where you want to be. The first thing I had to realise, was that Plan A sometimes had to wait and Plan B implemented because bills had to be paid and kids had to be fed. But if you worked hard enough, and got more qualified (instead of just Authorised by the SIA!), and had a bit of luck on your side, then your dream of doing the job you want to do, really can materialise. But hey, guess what? No one will knock on your door and ask you to come and work for them; it's now a full time job to find a job!

So, with this all in mind, let's talk about training and further training offered to protection personnel once they have completed their initial basic SIA training course.

Now we have all seen the influx of training companies

that offer training in close protection, and who have instructors form what seems to be the biggest Regiment in the British Army (the SAS) because everyone whose an instructor seems to have served in it! But in reality, when you get to the course it's nothing like what you expected and the instruction is laughable and the instructor is some ex-security guard who has a Teacher Training Qualification and lied through his back-teeth about his operational experience (please believe me when I say that the awarding bodies never check, they just want the money). As long there are people wanting a licence to work, there are companies willing to supply the training, regardless of whether it is good training or not.

      Professional companies though, are more rigorous with their selection and they look at the training company that delivered the training, and the backgrounds of the instructors, as well as your Professional Career Development (this is what makes you professional instead of just authorised). So take a look at what courses you have done in your little PCD folder; most of you will have a copy of your SIA Licence, a copy of your basic training CP course and hopefully a First Aid certificate, but I would say that most people with just these in their folder are now driving a bus or digging holes or stacking shelves for a living, and never got a reply to the two thousand or so CVs they sent out and then wonder why aren't they working in CP? Because ladies and gentlemen, you are in the 'Authorised Only' zone and this industry has moved on over the years and now you must move into the 'Professional' zone, or get left behind. The SIA say that you can work if you have a licence, but this makes you authorised only, and certainly not Professional (but they also say you can work the door on this licence without any Physical Intervention Training too! Enough said about the SIA).

      So what makes you Professional and gives you more chance of landing that contract.

      If you knock on my door with the following qualifications then the kettle is on:

For UK:
1. SIA Licence.
2. CP Certificate from a reputable Company.
3. Level 3 FAW or/MIRA/FPOSI.
4. Handcuff Qualification.
5. Physical Intervention/Disengagement Qualification.
6. Advanced Driving or Car Jockey Qualification.

For Hostile/Overseas:
1. SIA Licence.
2. MIRA/FPOSI.
3. Handcuff.
4. Physical.
5. Anti ambush/Evasive Driving Course.
6. Weapons Trained.

This is my opinion as an employer who has over three hundred professional CPOs on my books and, at times, have had over one hundred and fifty men on the ground. This, for me anyway, is what being being qualified is all about.

Let's look at a typical company close protection vacancy advert:

Job Introduction:
G4S Risk Management is the specialist protective security and consulting arm of G4S plc, the world's leading international security solutions group and a FTSE 100 listed company. It builds on the comprehensive experience and the global expertise of G4S, with its 600,000 employees and an annual turnover in excess of £5 billion. G4S Risk Management provides a range of services for clients operating in complex or sensitive environments. G4S Risk Management's primary focus is to provide national governments, multinational corporations and international peace and security agencies operating in hostile or sensitive environments with:

- *Protective security services*

- Risk advisory and consultancy services
- Specialist training
- Mine action services including Weapons Reduction and Explosive Ordnance Management
- Development and reconstruction services.

We are continually recruiting for CP Operators to work at the front end of the delivery of our operation, the role requires individuals people who are suitably experienced and qualified in firearms and armoured vehicle driving, they must be able to follow instructions clearly but also able to make command decisions on the spot in order to achieve the aims of the organization. We have operations in Afghanistan on a rotation of 9 weeks in-country, 3 weeks on leave. This is subject to a 12 month service agreement.

Role Responsibility:

- *Provide Close Protection in accordance with SOP's for all clients as directed during Ops briefs or other "Quick Orders" briefs to take positive action and accountability for assigned work.*
- *To assist the CPO Team Leader to execute the day to day assigned tasks.*
- *To assist the Vehicle Commander in prior and post mission administration for serviceability and accountability of all designated equipment.*
- *To provide statements when requested for the preparation of all incidents and accident reports.*
- *To maintain a high standard of welfare, morale and discipline.*
- *Execute any other tasks commensurate to the Operator's role as deemed appropriate by the Project Manager.*
- *Maintain a professional operational relationship with the clients.*
- *Maintain an acceptable level of physical fitness.*

The Ideal Candidate:
- *To be considered for these roles candidate CV's MUST be able to demonstrate the following:*
- *Formal military / police training with at least 7 years' service.*
- *Recognised Close Protection course and current SIA licence in Frontline Close Protection.*
- *Recent experience in a volatile or relevant environment (active service / commercial experience in low infrastructure environments). Experience of firearms / off-road driving / first aid. Excellent communication skills and the ability to follow instructions.*

So when you look at this, why would employers take on authorised instead of qualified staff, especially as they are also under pressure from the insurance companies to take on the right staff or any potential claim could go out the window?

So, if you really want a career in close protection, look very carefully at other training courses that are available to enhance your Professional Career Development, and only do the courses you need to do, without wasting time and money on training that you will never need or use. And remember, there are lots of sharks out there with Teacher Qualifications but who have never work in the role that they are teaching, so spend your money wisely too!

SHOULD CPOs BE TRAINED IN CQC?
By Robin Barratt

This is a question that those who have extensive unarmed combat training will unreservedly say; *"of course!"* and those with no training and who are too lazy to train will obviously say; *"no, unarmed combat training is irrelevant for the modern CPO."*

Personally I absolutely believe that every single protection officer should not only be trained in unarmed combat, but be experts in unarmed combat! I cannot and will never understand the irrational, stupid philosophy of some people working in this sector - I believe that if you cannot disarm, disable and defend against an opponent, then you should not be looking after the safety of others. Period. And it doesn't matter whether you are in the UK or in Russia. Try telling a Russian bodyguard that you don't have any combat experience, he will laugh his head off!

The arguments put forward by those without any combat training are varied and include that if a protection officer plans his operation carefully and properly, looking at and countering every single possible risk, then there would never be any need for any physical confrontation or intervention so then why should a protection officer train for something he or she will probably never need? I agree; of course all operations should be planned meticulously, covering every possible eventuality, but this is an argument mainly made by the inexperienced and novice, because seasoned operatives will absolutely know it is never possible to counter every single eventuality, because you cannot ever fully plan against something that cannot be understood, and another person's thoughts, feelings, impulses or actions can never be completely understood. The fundamental objective of a CPO is to make things extremely difficult, if not impossible, for an attacker, but even with immense resources, manpower and capabilities, even the best security operations and organisations in the world have at times been breached; Presidents have been assassinated and top businessmen kidnapped. Attacks have often been made on impulse too, with no prior planning from the attacker. It happens. Fact. So what would an untrained CPO do if someone did impulsively jump over the barrier and run towards his or her film-star client at a film premier... run away? Of course most CPOs would try to stop them, but most would neither have the ability or facility to be able to, because they have never been trained to. As mentioned earlier, at a recent close protection training course I asked a class of students; *'who thinks they can look after themselves?'* Everyone put up their hand. I then asked who has actually had any extensive unarmed combat training? Only one person put up their hand. At another class I asked the same question and again everyone put up their hand, I then took a fake knife out and attacked two or three students, no one could defend themselves... actually no one even made any attempt to! This type of bodyguard training is fully endorsed by the Security Industry Authority and the British Government, and therefore because of this, CPOs actually think it is OK not to be trained. Listen carefully... it is not! Sadly this will only be made public when someone famous is either injured or killed in an attack because their bodyguards failed to protect them.

  I have also heard an argument saying that the UK and the USA are still very different when it comes to violence and the use of weapons and firearms; people in the US have a constitutional right to bare arms and therefore they are much more widely used than here in the UK. I agree, but this is of course completely irrelevant to the role of the CPO. People get shot and stabbed in the UK each and every day of the year, so therefore regardless of the fact that more people in the US than in the UK have guns, the actual risk of weapons being used is exactly the same. And just because we don't have as many guns in circulation here in the UK, kitchens are still full of knives! The risks are still there, and therefore by default training in disarming techniques should be part of every bodyguard's ongoing training programme, wherever you live.

  I also heard one very stupid CPO argue that putting someone down in an attack could result in a prosecution of the bodyguard! This was his genuine argument for not training in unarmed combat, he didn't want to get arrested if ever he had to use his training countering an attack. Yes, I know, hard to believe that someone in this business and with an SIA licence actually thinks this way. My reply was simple... firstly don't be a bodyguard if you think that you might get arrested for doing your job and secondly, an untrained, unskilled bodyguard is actually likely to do more damage and could possibly go too far in order to compensate for their lack of skills than someone skilled and trained. To disarm and disable an attacker in a controlled and efficient manner, or to kick the shit out of someone in untrained and uncontrolled manner; I am not a legal expert but I am sure a court would favour the first.

Also, if a five-man BG team consisted of only one unarmed combat trained BG, if an attack did occur and the trained BG was disabled, what then? Not only is the client, but the whole team is at risk.

Someone recently said to me that they have been working in close protection for almost ten years and have not trained, nor will ever train in any form of unarmed combat. Their reason is because nothing has ever happened and they plan each operation so well they are confident nothing will ever happen. I think this attitude is completely wrong. They just have to pray to whatever God they believe in, that nothing will ever happen because it would be too late for me to then say; *'I told you so,'* wouldn't it ?

I wonder how many of the thousands of UK SIA licensed CPOs, and the tens of thousands of CPOs worldwide can honestly put their hand on their hearts and say they have the training necessary to counter an attack on their client if ever an attack occurred. Probably very few. How many are arrogant enough to say they don't need unarmed combat training, probably quite a few!

I have been very lucky in my career both in security and protection, as well as a writer and author, and have travelled the world meeting BGs from many countries including the USA, South America, The Balkans, Russia (and many other eastern European countries), and, almost all are tough men and experts in unarmed combat. The best bodyguards are undoubtedly the best trained, so if you want to be one of the best, get yourself fully trained and don't make excuses for your own inadequacies.

CQC, A MUST FOR THE PROFESSIONAL CPO
By Tyrrel Francis

You are a Close Protection Operative, part of a team of six, escorting your client - a respected Middle Eastern Sheik, back to his hotel at the end of a long day of engagements. You have worked for the Sheik before and found him to be a generous and likeable man, with lots of supporters, both in his home country, and in the West. He does, however, have a small contingent of haters connected to extreme groups, hence the need for a close protection contract with your firm.

You are met by the usual crowd of admirers as you approach the hotel, turning out to show their appreciation of the Sheik's work. This is good for public relations, but a security headache for you, so you are on your guard as you and your team exit the vehicles and form a tight cordon. The Sheik, not wishing to appear arrogant or unappreciative, takes time to meet the public, under the watchful eyes of you and your team in the stifling heat. You have done this many times, and so far there has not been a problem. You ignore the sweat running down the back of your neck as you scan the crowd for threats, eyes protected from the glare of the sun by your sunglasses. Then your trained eye spots a man breaking away from the crowd, picking the weakest point in your perimeter. All that stands in his way, as he sprints towards the Sheik, shouting fanatically in his native tongue, is you.

He closes the distance as you step into his path, shouting a warning - a pre-agreed codeword to warn your team that you have a contact. He is on you before you can draw your side arm, only meters from your client and the well-wishing crowd, who have not yet reacted to the danger. He runs straight into you, and you take hold of him. In that instant you recognise the look of a man who has nothing to lose, and is willing to die for his cause. He shouts and spits at you as you struggle, close enough to smell his tobacco breath and body odour. In your peripheral vision you see your colleagues ushering the Sheik away from danger, as you fight to restrain the attacker, who, seeing his target moving away from him, reaches inside his local traditional clothes. Your trained mind recognises the danger, relegating all thoughts of self-preservation and the family for whom you carry out this lucrative but potentially dangerous work, as the attacker reaches for what could be a weapon, or more likely, a means of blowing himself up, taking you, the Sheik, your colleagues and some of the crowd with him.

When you applied for a job as a Close Protection Operative, did the firm you were applying to insist that you already have an unarmed skills base, and if so, what criteria did they specify? Some form of training is provided, due to the nature of your chosen profession, but how much emphasis can your firm put on Close Quarter Combat, when there are a range of skills in which to become competent, in a relatively short space of time. Surely, prerequisite or not, it is easier to simply add whatever techniques you learn for the job, to an existing skills base. It is just a case of which one.

Ju Jitsu

If you have are well-practised in this art, then you have a very good, compatible base to work from, with a range of both defensive and controlling techniques to draw from, which are very compatible with other Close Quarter techniques. Just be careful if you are looking at starting the art to help your application as, like many ancient martial arts, Ju Jitsu has many styles, and some, such as Brazilian Ju Jitsu, have greater emphasis on the ground fighting and grappling aspect, which are useful to have as a backup, but for Close Protection you need to be working from your feet as much as possible.

Aikido

Like Judo, Aikido has its roots in Ju Jitsu, but unlike Judo, it was based around the standing techniques, with the strikes and wrist locks included, as well as the throws, and has a spiritual, meditation aspect similar to Tai Chi. An experienced and well drilled Aikido practitioner has a useful and relevant arsenal of techniques for control and immobilisation to call upon, but again, it is not an art which you can just pick up and put into practice in six months, even a year, so if you are considering this art, it is best to find a good club and take it up well before your application is submitted to a Close Protection firm, and like any art, it will have to be maintained and progressed.

Krav Maga
This system evolved from the Israeli military, and offers a range or useful techniques and drills. The nature and experience offered from the origin of this art make it a very relevant skills base to work from for Close Quarter Combat.

Wing Chun
The close range anticipation and trapping drills practised in this art can be very compatible with control and restraint techniques. Practising this art will build up your intuitive skills, both with a view to anticipating your adversary's actions, but countering them.

Combat Sports Systems
It may be that you are a practitioner of a combat sport such as Boxing, Kickboxing, Wrestling, Muay Thai or Mixed Martial Arts. None of these will be specific training for Close Quarter Combat, because the objective is different. However, you may find that they fit in nicely with the role specific techniques that you have learned, and that the hours of training and practice with opponents and sparring partners can be beneficial when faced with the sudden need to struggle with somebody intent on doing you, your colleagues and your client, harm.

The S.P.E.A.R. System
This system was patented by Canadian Martial Artist Tony Blauer, after he conducted an experiment with the assistance of his students. He asked them to stand in a circle around him, and to attack him randomly with whichever technique they wished, in

any order they wished. He found that when he attempted to use a variety of blocks for different attacks, he failed to deflect the attacks. During the exercise, he notice that his body naturally reverted to its instinctive flinch reaction, which triggered the same primal response, lifting the arms to protect the head, moving the body's core away from the threat, and dropping into a stance, and that this gave him the highest success rate in defending against the varies attacks. He called the system "S.P.E.A.R.", Spontaneous Protecting Enabling Accelerated Response, trademarked the name and sold it to the US. The system is now used by military and law enforcement worldwide for many applications, and could even be included in your training provided for Close Protection. One of the advantages of S.P.E.A.R. is that it fits in well with other systems, and as a basic principle, is simple enough to be functional without hours of weekly training dedicated it, as it is based on the body's natural instinct to protect itself.

You could argue that the opening paragraph is an extreme case, and that statistically, the amount of time that a Close Protection Operative spends in Close Quarter Combat is a very small percentage, compared to putting the other skills into practice. And that in very hostile and dangerous environments, such as The Middle east and Africa, personal weapons and other equipment would be kept closer to hand and in a state of readiness. Close Protection is a team profession, so again, your colleagues will assist you, but only once the safety of your client is assured, and they will be relying on you to give them vital moments to do this. You could argue that proper planning and preparation should be carried out and this type of scenario avoided. This also, may be true. But Close Protection is such a diverse profession, covering a wide range of clientele and environments. You could be protecting high profile sports stars or musicians one week, foreign dignitaries the next, and then high-risk business people, and not every situation can be planned for. Therefore, surely it is better to have muscle memory from regular training in some form of unarmed combat, even if it is not specifically for your job role.

You will know what you will and won't be able to use, as it is the same principle as not attempting a head kick when in grappling range during an MMA bout, and you will instinctively favour the relevant techniques. This can only come from regular training, as a periodic refresher session every month, six months, year or however long, cannot match 2-3 times a week or more sustained throughout, which also has the added advantage of keeping you in good health and fitness, and relieving the stress of a hard and demanding profession.

***

Tyrrel Francis' book **Personal Safety & Self Defence - A practical guide to avoiding and dealing with conflict,** *is out now in paperback ISBN: 978-1514889855 and Kindle ASIN: B011ANAQ18. This essential little book contains lots of useful tips and hints on how to avoid becoming a victim of violent crime, as well as how to recognise and anticipate potential trouble. It also gives practical suggestions for dealing with difficult situations and escaping danger, as well as a simple guide to staying on the right side of the law.*

CQC FOR PROTECTION OFFICERS
By Mo Teague

For the purposes of this chapter Close Quarter Combat (CQC) is defined as; *"The unarmed and armed (hand held/shoulder fired weapon) combative skills that take place within a confined space or within limited range (30 feet) between individuals/small teams."*

Working in a hostile environment poses many challenges to the modern protection officer, most of which are logistical by nature and involve hours of preparation and planning to minimise and negate any and all possible likely threats to a client and protection assets. With advances in relevant technology, protection methods and procedures utilising high-tech equipment have enhanced survivability, although it can be argued that is has also rendered 'old school' physical skills redundant. For many it's as much about balancing the finances as it is about efficiency; training = time = money. Physical training skill development takes time, so in many cases and for many people training is compressed and compromised to the point of being meaningless, the emphasis being on technical skills and not on actual real-life events. And so, it all comes down to individuals personally taking the initiative by accessing quality training providers and resources, and investing both time and money to learn and develop practical real world physical survival skills.

History and modern anecdotal evidence proves that, at close range, there is no substitute for solid CQB skills aligned with a robust, resilient physical and mental capacity. These skills however are not acquired easily and many hours must be spent in not only acquiring them, but also in maintaining them to a standard to which they can be utilised - if and when necessary. As always in these matters it comes down to three things:

- **Time**
- **Money**
- **Motivation**

Time

"I don't have time" is the plea I hear time and time again, to which the answer is always that we all have the same number of hours in a day and that its not about making more time - which is obviously impossible - but about good time-management. If you want to do something badly enough you will find a way, otherwise you will find an excuse; put the same amount of integrity into planning personal professional development as you would into operational planning and organise and schedule CQC training into your personal professional development plan (you do have one don't you?) And then do the work. The bottom line is; if you don't have time now, you certainly won't have time in a potentially lethal close quarter encounter.

Money

Money, like time, is a commodity no-one has enough of and similarly must be organised and scheduled as part of your finance plan (budget). Good CQC can be relatively expensive, especially if you have to factor in travel, food, accommodation costs etc., and is a specialist subject in its own right. However an interim consideration would be a relevant martial art or sport such as Muay Thai, MMA, boxing, judo etc., and whilst these can be utilised short-term and valuable to develop attributes, they do not possess the tactical skills and knowledge of a valid CQC program. Train with the best you can afford; it may mean sacrifice in other areas but it's an investment that will add value to your CV and may save your life!

Motivation

It is imperative that a protection officer has the full confidence in himself and that of his colleagues, client / employer. A quiet confidence portrayed through a confident professional demeanour gives not only a discernible message to colleagues and fellow professionals, but also to those whose intent is to harm, and it should be noted that almost all attacks are pre-ceded by hostile surveillance. Confidence comes from a total belief in the validity of one's training and ability to perform under extreme circumstances; the base for that confidence is the base that gives the other skills tactical context.

The close protection world is a relatively small one where reputation counts for everything and can determine not only whether you are employed but at what level and for how much. Reputation is gained through performance standards.

"I am a member of a profession which is unique in the scope and severity of the consequences of incompetence in its practice. I therefore strive single mindedly to achieve the highest degree of proficiency achievable in the practice of my professional arts"

Hard Target Code of Ethics
Motivation = standards + performance + confidence = reputation = work = money.

"Your belief in what is possible and the standards you set and hold for yourself will determine what action you take and the results you will get"

Integration
CQC is not a stand-alone skill-set, but should be integrated as part of the whole training and operational ethos, which is defined and determined by the threat; actual or implied. A threat is considered in terms of probability and consequences and, whilst in most cases an attack on a client or protection team is unlikely, the consequences of such an attack can be devastating, life changing and even life-ending. Attacks at close range are sudden, employing deception and the element of surprise, and are highly aggressive. Attackers will quickly close the range to deploy firearms and/or edged weapons, and it is at this time that those

hours of investment in terms of time, money, blood sweat and tears pays off. Violence is not an abstract notion, when it happens it's real; don't be wise after the event…. if you're still alive. Train now!

Summary

Training in CQC:

- **Enhances survivability.**
- **Enhances professional integrity and reputation.**
- **Enhances confidence.**
- **Enhances employability.**
- **Gives tactical context to other skills.**

For further information contact Mo Teague via email: moteague@hotmail.co.uk or call: + 44 7976841935.

AN INTERESTING CONVERSATION
By Robin Barratt

On a recent brief visit to the US, I met up with a good friend who is undoubtedly one of the most experienced protectors in the USA, if not the world. I shall call him Brad. Brad has worked in close protection continuously since the '70s and, as a member of the US Government Service, has worked operationally in senior protective roles for a number of US Presidents, both in the USA and worldwide. He has also protected a large number of visiting dignitaries, including other Presidents, Prime Ministers and Royalty. Now retired from government service, Brad now works full-time for one of the most respected and reputed security consultancy companies in the US. He still sets up and manages major security operations, as well as instructs all new employees. On top of this, Brad is also a best-selling author and has written some brilliant books on the industry. There is little he doesn't know about the protection industry, although he willingly testifies that he still has so much more to learn - which kind of puts into perspective those idiots in the UK who think they know it all after just a couple of weeks training and an SIA badge!

Anyway, among the many things we chatted about were the changes with close protection and training here in the UK, and how almost overnight the British government changed what was once an elite industry of well-trained professionals into a job literally open to almost everyone. When I told him that, at the start of licensing, the SIA had not made any form of self-defence, control and restraint or unarmed combat training compulsory he almost fell off his seat laughing! When I told him there were well over fifteen thousand licensed close protection operatives in the UK, with probably about 80% having no unarmed combat or self-defence skills whatsoever, he was then visibly shocked. Actually, he didn't believe me! He thought I was pulling his leg. When he asked me what psychological vetting and controls were in place for hopeful CPOs, I said that apart from a criminal record check currently in the UK there are no other vetting requirements to get a licence to protect someone else's life. When he asked if fitness was a factor in training, I told him no; you can be totally unfit, hugely overweight, have no self-defence training, be unable to drive and, before attending a course, sweep streets or stack supermarket shelves, and yet still get a British Government approved licence to operate as a Close Protection Officer in the UK. Blood drained from his face. He thought either I, or the British Government (or both!), were completely mad.

"How can the British Government license protectors that are simply unable to protect?" he asked unbelievingly. *"And how can the British Government accredit a protection course which simply does not prepare anyone, in any way, with the skills required to protect?"*

I told him that I thought that when licensing for CPOs was first introduced into the UK, the government and the Security Industry Authority placed total and absolute emphasis on advance training and conflict management skills, but omitted many of the other key and immensely important skills that are most certainly required for protection officers when things don't always go to plan. They stupidly and naively thought that with even the basic skills, most situations could be resolved effectively.

"I totally and absolutely agree with the SIA in the provision of comprehensive advance training; it will and does save many lives and dissuades many, many attacks. Proper advance work is the fundamental key to any form of protection, but what about those few situations that cannot and do not dissuade or stop an attack?" he asked. *"What does the SIA expect protectors to do in a situation, for instance, at a film premier in Leicester Square, with cameras flashing and celebrities everywhere, and some nutter with a grudge jumping over the barrier and charging towards your client with a knife? Two protectors are ahead of your client and see him running towards them. With no training, what are they to do, try to talk him out of it?"* He laughs; *"Perhaps they are taught to turn and run away?"* More laughter as he imagines bodyguards running away, hands flapping in the air, screaming. After recovering, he continues

seriously; *"Or perhaps, because this has probably never happened in the UK, why then train for something that may never happen? Or perhaps your so-called conflict management trainers and instructors have never actually been in such a situation themselves, so therefore they don't have the appropriate skills to instruct others. Or maybe they simply instruct protectors not to protect if the dangers are just too great?"* A worried and confused look crossed his face. *"But seriously, protectors will have to tackle the attacker, and of course will have to disarm him and take him to the ground while the other protectors evacuate your client, but with no training or skills in weapon disarmament this is both suicidal for the protectors and, what is worse, possible extremely dangerous for your client - as with little or no training the attacker could quite easily disable the protectors and continue with his (or her) mission."*

I thought he was absolutely right; perhaps the SIA had hoped that this sort of an attack would never ever happen in the UK! I then went onto tell him the sad fact that all British contractors and employers now ask for an SIA license when employing protectors and even the most respected, biggest and most recognised UK contractors actively demand that its personnel have SIA licenses, even though they know that the training is inadequate. Even now, years after SIA licensing was first introduced, many companies still use the SIA badge as a lever to tender for contracts, even though they know full well that, in a close quarter emergency and attack situation, many, if not most, SIA badged personnel actually have little or no CQB experience or training. In all my years in the industry, I have never once seen an application form for a CP position which asks the candidate to list his or her self-defence / CQB skills. Not once! I have never seen an advertised position that lists extensive self-defence / CQB skills in the job description and I have never heard of an employer testing the self-defence / CQB skills of its applicants. This never, ever happens in the UK.

"This is unbelievable!" Brad said. *"So protectors can apply and quite possibly get a job as a protector without have any actual skills of physical protection?"*

Embarrassingly I had to agree.

"So, by British law, do training companies have to have accreditation from the SIA to teach close protection?" he asked.

I replied by confirming that all companies in the UK that wish to teach close protection have to be accredited as training providers by the SIA.

"So why doesn't SIA accredited training companies offer extensive training in unarmed combat, even though it is not part of the SIA accreditation, but knowing that it is a fundamental requirement and responsibility of professional protection?" Brad asked, trying to get his head around this concept of protectors not actually being able to physically protect and the UK Government allowing, in fact endorsing this to happen.

I explained that, because of costs and the commercialisation of CP training, many training companies here in the UK are simply not at all interested in training professional Close Protection Officers, but only in making money. A longer course would cost more money, and training companies now fight hard to compete with the many other close protection training companies offering the same basic training. And sadly there are also many, many Close Protection Officers wanting the cheapest and easiest route into the industry, regardless of the standards of their initial training. If one course was advertised for £1500 for two weeks, and the other £2500 for three weeks but also included one full week of unarmed combat and disarming - yet the SIA badge will be the same at the end - sadly most students will still take the first option.

"But surely close protection training in the UK - the actual training of someone to protect another person's life - is only carried out by a select few elite training companies?" He asked.

On the contrary, I had to reply sadly. I told him that with commercialisation, more or less anyone can now open a close protection training company in the UK, because as a trainer you do not actually need to have any form of experience in close protection, you just need a teaching certificate! There is no government or official vetting and verification of actual CP experience; as long as you don't have a criminal record, can follow the basic syllabus, can prove your status as a teacher with a basic teaching qualification, you can teach close protection. In theory, you do not actually have to have one day's close protection experience to be able to teach close protection!

"But this is complete madness," he exclaimed. "What about further accrediting of the trainers?" he asked, "perhaps an exclusive endorsed accreditation system for trainers offering a much higher standard of training than the basic training requirements of the SIA, For example; Members of the Elite Trainer Association...just an idea," he suggests.

I agreed, yes it would be a great idea, and then CPOs training with a company whose trainers are members of this elite association would know that their training would be far superior than XYZ company with know-nothing trainers in nowhere town, and also of course contractors would also know that candidates coming from these elite schools would be so much better. But many UK training companies would say; Why? Even if the SIA does not guarantee any real standard or level of close protection training, they have their SIA accreditation as trainers anyway so why on earth would they need another accreditation? They would also ask why should UK training companies offer extra training at an extra cost which is not needed for the SIA licence anyway? I did add that of course there are a few very well recognised, well respected training companies with higher than average standards, and of course there are many very good CP instructors with lots of operational experience out there too, but the subject of this conversation was discussing the fact that the British Government has also accredited the average, below average and appalling – both instructors and CPOs!

"This is very interesting and extraordinarily revealing," he said. "I have worked with you Brits on many, many occasions while I was in the US Government service, and many times since. We looked after Margaret Thatcher on her visits to the US, as well as many other of your dignitaries and officials. You Brits were probably some of the most professional protectors I have ever had the pleasure of working with... unlike some of us Yanks"

Brad winked and laughed. *"You were always so conservative and polite and had exact and extremely high standards. It seems things have changed, it seems that now in the UK anyone can train to be a protector and anyone train protectors even if they have no experience in the field protecting themselves, which to me seems to contradict the whole idea behind the SIA and the idea of professionalising the industry."*

I assured him that even now, regardless of how the industry has changed, most full-time UK bodyguards are still originally from the Special Forces, Royal Military Police or Diplomatic Security, or with other strong military or police backgrounds. There are also many civilian protectors that completely understand that an SIA badge is just the first of many steps, and go onto develop a strong portfolio of further training including extensive CQB training. But, in my opinion, by making the industry open to anyone regardless of experience or background, aptitude or intelligence, and by making close protection training available to almost anyone, this has not raised standards of CP in the UK at all, but has in fact significantly lowered them. And this is not just my opinion, but the opinion of almost all of the true professionals in this industry. There are now many, many more wannabes on the Circuit than ever.

"I think I must agree with you." Brad replied. *"Although I can see how some individuals and training companies in the UK would disagree with you; money and profit often transcends decency and doing what is right! It is much, much harder to set up a security training company in the US, and not easy to get a bodyguard license to protect either. Although I have to say there are also a great many protectors here in the US too that definitely should not be protecting! They are relying on luck rather than skill, and of course there are many US protectors working in high-risk theatres like Iraq who, because of their un-professionalism, have given the majority of bodyguards an appalling name and reputation. Sadly though, this happens everywhere in the world and in almost every industry, not just close protection. But if individually we say to ourselves that we will do the very best we possibly can, be completely professional*

and absolutely believe in what we do, things can – and will – get better and being a protector will once again be an honourable, ethical and worthy profession."

CERTIFICATION AND EXPERIENCE
By Tony Scotti

Two topics of discussions that dominate the social media, both here in the US and worldwide, are certification and the state of the training in the protection industry. In reality the two subjects cannot be separated. The job market wants, and will support, a certification that meets the standards set by respected industry and government organizations. Those who supply job opportunities welcome an Certification that will withstand the scrutiny of the corporate, legal and insurance community. However, that being said, there are still job markets in the protection business globally where insurance risk and liability are not a concern, and neither is certification.

Many of the protection practitioners, both new and old to the business that desire certification, do not have a clear understanding of the concept of certification as defined by most other industries. That is in a large part because of the insane number of Bodyguard/EP training providers who use the word *certification* as a marketing tool, with no real idea of what it means. This is the same in the UK as it is in the US, with UK bodyguard schools offering SIA certification with no real understanding what being a *first class* protector really means.

Most of the practitioners feel that if they attend a training program, and the training provider says they are certified – well they are certified. When told, no that is not certification with regards to real-life protection, it evokes a myriad of verbiage, usually none pleasant.

The general feeling in the industry is - *"I have spent all this time and money to attend training programs, of course I am certified"* – well that is not how the concept of certification works.

Training and Certification
In other industries it is common practice to conduct training and

issue a certificate. That is a reasonable and accepted practice, which is evident by the number of certified seminars and events that cover a particular industry subject. But it is not the same as certification. So this has to be said – for decades, particularly in the the US and in many other countries worldwide, the CP training available is not certification - it is training to a certificate – there is an enormous difference, which does not mean that the certificate is not valuable – but it is not a certification as defined by the accrediting organizations that are the standards in many other industries. And that is the key issue; if the EP/CP industry wants to be recognized by the job market as creditable and professional, the industry has to do what other industries do – be recognized by credentialing organizations.

The major issue that seems to be problematic is experience vs certification. This may be hard to accept – but you cannot enter a training program with little or no experience and at the end of five, seven, or whatever days later and be certified by those who have conducted the training, In fact it is ludicrous to think you can have a certification without experience, and in fact so does the job market.

The question becomes; can the industry survive without a certification that is universally recognized and meets the strictest definition. The answer is... yes. It has survived for decades and will continue to survive. But in the final word; what is the definition of survive? Survive, in my eyes anyway, means the individual makes a living supplying protective services.

MAKING SURE YOU ARE INSURED
Interview with Freda West

Tell me about Camberford Law and when was your first security policy?
Camberford Law Plc was established in 1958 and has become highly regarded within the commercial insurance industry as a scheme specialist insurance broker. Whilst we understand quality of cover and pricing are very important to our clients we believe our strongest selling point is our customer focused approach to business. Our very first security policy was issued in the mid 1980s for a manned guarding company called Pegasus Security Ltd.

Tell me about the different policies you provide the security sector and how do you define their specific needs?
Concentrating in particular sectors we undertake substantial research in order to determine the needs of our customers and translate this into policy covers with consistently competitive premiums. Each scheme is handled by a specialist team of insurance professionals dedicated to offering our clients insurance cover to meet the needs of their business. The largest of our schemes has been carefully put together in order to provide comprehensive insurance cover specific to the needs of the Security Industry. Cover can apply to Manned Guarding companies, Training companies (e.g. Physical Intervention and Survival Techniques), Alarm, CCTV & Fire Extinguisher Installers, Door Supervisors, Event Stewards, Security Consultancy & Assessment companies and of course Close Protection companies. In fact, we provide insurance for all types and sizes of client, ranging from one man bands to the largest corporate clients and the principles are basically the same, as are the policy wordings and covers. Although many of our clients operate only in the UK and Europe, we can arrange worldwide cover if necessary.

What about Employers' Liability and Public Liability?

Employers' Liability is statutory in the UK if the company has employees (subject to certain exclusions), and Public Liability is also provided, starting at a minimum indemnity limit of £2,000,000. Our Close Protection policies tend to start at a PL limit of £5,000,000. An important extension to the Public Liability cover is efficacy (also known as inefficacy). This is simply explained as 'the failure to carry out a duty or service that an insured or contractor performs in the course of his business'. This could be the failure of a product, such as an alarm not activating, therefore allowing a break-in to a client's premises. In the case of a Close Protection Officer, an example would be if a CPO is protecting someone in a large crowd and a gun went off and injured their client, this would be covered as it would be outside the control of the officer.

What other policies do you provide?

We also arrange professional indemnity insurance, travel insurance including repatriation, kidnap and ransom, personal accident, life and medical insurances.

How do you rate a specific insurance policy?

When rating a policy and calculating the premium we take many risk factors into account, such as the particular security sector, geographical areas visited, and experience of our policyholders. We also need financial information such as a company's estimated annual turnover and wage roll or payments to sub-contractors. We operate in a very discreet and confidential manner in accordance with the terms of the 1998 Data Protection Act and would not disclose or discuss any of our clients; we are only able to mention Pegasus Security as that company was subsequently taken over.

What should anyone in the security sector look for when choosing an insurer?

When choosing an insurance provider, clients should look for experience in their particular sector and financial strength in the insurer; we only use A rated insurers or higher. We have various composite and Lloyd's markets that we use to place cover for our security industry clients, so we are not tied to one particular insurer.

Should a claim need to be made, how is this done?
We have an in-house claims department with many years' collective experience and they try to make the claim process as pain-free as possible, during what can sometimes be a stressful time for our clients. Clients are guided through the notification process and we will liaise with the insurance company as much (or as little) as necessary on their behalf. We issue all policy documents in-house by email with a very speedy turnaround and can arrange for payments to be made by monthly instalments.

How do I find out more information?
We are well known as insurance providers within the security industry and we make every effort to maintain our high standards, and we always welcome new enquiries and pride ourselves on customer service. So for more information and to discuss your specific requirements in complete confidence, please contact us: T: +44 (0) 20 8315 5022, E-mail: FredaW@camberfordlaw.com or via the website: www.camberfordlaw.com

LASTLY... HAS THE GOVERNMENT FAILED THE BRITISH CLOSE PROTECTION INDUSTRY?

As we all know, anyone entering the Close Protection industry in the United Kingdom must have a license to operate as a CPO, and the only way to get a license is to attend a training course accredited by the SIA. Once you have attended and passed one of these courses, you can then apply for your licence at a further costs of £220 every three years (as of 2014). Established in 2003, The Security Industry Authority (SIA) was set up *"to raise standards of professionalism and skills within the private security industry and to promote and spread best practice"*. It reports directly to the British Government's Home Office, and its remit is *"to help protect society by collaboratively developing and achieving high standards within the private security industry"*. However as we discussed in the previous chapters, in my opinion, specifically within the Close Protection sector, it has done just the opposite.

I'll be honest with you; I really do agree with licensing for CPOs, and I also totally agree with really good training, accountability and transparency within this specific sector of security. However, in the Government's quest to control everything and everyone, and an irresponsible and irrational commercialisation of the security industry, in my opinion it has made the close protection industry frighteningly more dangerous for both operators and, more importantly, the clients themselves. What was once a unique, elite industry manned by some of the best trained professional operatives in the world, is now open to absolutely anyone - and I mean anyone! Now anyone from any background can get a license and therefore an endorsement by the British Government to 'protect' another human being against the threat of assault, kidnap and ultimately assassination. You can be an over-weight, unfit, mentally unstable 18 year old supermarket shelf-filler, who cannot even drive a car and who has not done one minute of exercise and has no knowledge of self-defence, and yet still attend and pass a British Government approved close protection training course and apply for - and receive - a Government endorsed front-line license in Close Protection. In my opinion, this is not making the industry more professional, it has turned the British close protection industry into a global laughing stock.

Admittedly, like every industry, before the SIA there were the cowboys; people running correspondence courses in close protection, farcical fitness-based courses run by people with absolutely no CP experience whatsoever, and so-called CP courses based entirely on unarmed combat. And admittedly, the SIA has rid the industry of most of these clowns, but it has replaced them with something a lot more sinister. Prior to the SIA, the industry was pretty much self-governing; contracts were awarded to operatives almost always via recommendations and referrals, and only to those that had attended intensive and extensive peer recognised training. So by default, the standards were going to be very high. And these peer recognised training companies never accepted people on their course that were not of a high calibre, and they never passed those who did not make the grade, regardless of how much they had paid for their course! Yes, it was unfortunate for those wannabe shelf-fillers that had wasted their hard-earned dosh, but the industry is ultimately there to protect clients against the gravest of threats, and not for feeling sorry for the wannabes who have wasted their money on a training course. Now, however, the sole priority for most close protection training companies is to pass as many students as possible, because who would pay for and attend a course with a training company that only had a 50% pass rate? Even if those 50% were the best of the best? Commercialisation of training has meant that in order for security training companies to survive, they must pass all their students, not because the level of instruction is so good that everyone passes, but solely because the student has paid for the course. I have seen adverts read: "100% pass rate guaranteed", "We will help you pass in as short time as possible," and even "money back guarantee, we will refund you if you do not pass." In my opinion, most training companies now are only motivated by profit, not by producing an elite team of professional bodyguards. This is what the SIA has done to the industry; it has opened it up to absolutely everyone and anyone, regardless of their background, experience or capabilities. They have given the job of protecting a client against a possible threat of assassination to absolutely anyone. There are many clients, contractors and employers that only ask whether you have an SIA licence, regardless of your background or experience. Let me give you one personal example: as I mentioned earlier, my speciality was high-risk protection in Russia. I have lived and worked in Moscow for many years, I got married in Russia and I had hundreds of local security-related contacts, yet I was once turned down for a job because the contractor was British and I did not have an SIA license - the job was given to someone with a license but who had never stepped foot in Russia. How is this of benefit to the principal? This is what the SIA has done.

I remember attending an SIA network meeting a while back and in an open Q&A forum I asked the SIA: if licensing was supposed to professionalise the industry, why can almost anyone pass an SIA course, surely this is a contradiction in terms? They had no answer.

However, there are still many good, honourable, experienced, professionals working within this industry sector, and this is what you must strive to be; to hold your head high and say to yourself 'I am bloody good at what I do.' Make it your goal to be an excellent CPO, but understand that being excellent at anything takes consistency, time and dedication, and being an excellent CPO is no exception. You will only get a good reputation if you know the job backwards and, like any job, the more you know the better you become, and the better you become the more professional you are, and the more professional you are the more powerful you are. Your first compulsory SIA training course should only be the beginning of a career in protection and, like any professional, you should develop your career by constantly learning, developing, experiencing and attending other training courses in particular self-defence, control and restraint, advanced first-aid, advanced conflict management and the full range of driver training. If you are serious about being a professional then you should be serious about gaining knowledge about the industry.

Aim to be the very best, and accept nothing less.

Seminars & Workshops

Based upon the content in this book. Robin Barratt holds **How To Find Work as a Close Protection Specialist** seminars and workshops to security training companies, groups and individuals anywhere in the world

For further information email: Robin@BarrattandAssociates.com

***

Coming shortly...

SECURITY & PROTECTION SERVICES IN THE RUSSIAN FEDERATION - A comprehensive guide to setting up and providing security services in the Russian Federation

To advertise in, and sponsor this publication and therefore reach thousands or potential clients within the corporate and celebrity sector email: Robin@BarrattandAssociates.com

Also by Robin Barratt Publishing...

BRITAIN'S TOUGHEST WOMEN - Some of the toughest women bodyguards, bouncers, bodybuilders, boxers, martial artists and MMA fighters in the UK

Britain's Toughest Women spotlights some of the toughest female bodyguards, bouncers, bodybuilders, boxers, martial artists and MMA fighters in the UK; women who live, work or play in a tough world.

Biography based chapters, looking at their past, present and plans for the future, what inspires and motivates them, and why they do what they do!

For some it's having a tough, challenging or traumatic upbringing, or feeling an underachiever at home or at school, or being bullied, or abused, or being pushed into things by their friends or family, or just overcoming life's challenges. For others it's solely their mindset and attitude, or simply following their dreams. It can be all sorts of things, and each person has their own, unique and fascinating story.

All the women featured here have chosen to be recognised for doing something exceptional and different; from working on the front-line in Iraq, to standing on stage as a competitive bodybuilder or entering the arena as an MMA fighter or boxer.

This book not only aims to spotlight these incredible women, but aims to motivate and inspire others, and to show that whatever background you're from, and whatever challenges and difficulties you've had, you can achieve too.

Paperback (6 inches x 9 inches - ISBN 978-1508941262) £9.99
Kindle (ASIN: B00WA7OT0S) £3.99

CONFESSIONS OF A DOORMAN
By Robin Barratt

Following on from the success of his best selling book Doing the Doors, doorman, bodyguard and martial arts expert Robin Barratt recalls more hard-hitting stories from his frequently violent life on nightclub doors around the UK. Barratt also records a few incredible and often hilarious takes from his time as a bodyguard in France, Russia and the Ukraine.

After being sent to clean up one of the most famous nightclubs in Paris, Barratt found himself 'hanging out' with a top Hollywood actor. In the Ukraine he came up against corrupt officials, and in Russia he worked alongside ex-Russian Special Forces. Confessions of a Doorman starts by chronicling his steroid related heart attack at the age of just 43.

Describing a lifetime of violence, turmoil and confusion, as well as his controversial opinions on the Security Industry Authority and his thoughts on what makes a first-rate doorman, Confessions is frequently comical, often shocking, occasionally heart-warming and written with Robin's usual style of pace, humour and honesty.

Paperback (6 inches x 9 inches – ISBN 978-1507754931) £9.99
Kindle (ASIN: B007WMX9KW) £3.99

www.RobinBarrattPublishing.com

Printed in Great Britain
by Amazon